THE LINE

A STORY OF A HUNTER, A BREED AND THEIR BOND

WILLIAM A. URSETH

ECW PRESS

Published by ECW Press
2120 Queen Street East, Suite 200, Toronto, Ontario, Canada M4E 1E2
416.694.3348 / info@ecwpress.com

LIBRARY AND ARCHIVES CANADA CATALOGUING IN PUBLICATION

Urseth, William A.
The line : a story of a hunter, a breed and their bond / William A. Urseth.

ISBN 978-1-55022-903-5

1. German shorthaired pointer. 2. Urseth, William A.
3. Fowling—United States. 4. Dog breeders—United
States—Biography. 5. Hunters—United States—Biography.
I. Title.

SF429.G4U78 2010   636.752'5   C2009-905927-4

Cover and Text Design: Tania Craan
Cover Image and Author Photo © Mike Urseth
Typesetting: Mary Bowness
Printing: Webcom   1   2   3   4   5

Interior images: pages ii, 1, 23, 30, 55, 60, 72, 77, 82, 101, 117, 133, 153, 181, 184, 194, 203 and 206, photos by Bill Urseth; pages 7 and 68, photos by Terry Holzinger; page 12 © Jarenwicklund /Dreamstime.com; page 17 © Iliuta Goean / Dreamstime.com; pages 38, 44, 103 and 211 reprinted courtesy of Menz Tournament Hunter magazine; pages 50, 241 and 245, photos by Mike Speer; pages 65, 86, 110, 114 and 128, photos by Peterson Portraits; pages 96, 139, 166, 173, 213, 247, 253, 270, 272 and 279, photos by Mike Urseth; pages 125, 145, 178, 188, 201, 264 and 267, photos by Mark Palas; page 150, photo by Ian Highway; page 160 © Karen Arnold / Dreamstime.com; pages 224, 256 and 261, photos by Randy Davis, RSD Photography; page 230, Prior Creative Images, LLC; page 233, © Matthew Veldhuis / Dreamstime.com.

PRINTED AND BOUND IN CANADA

ECW PRESS
ecwpress.com

Mixed Sources
Product group from well-managed
forests, and other controlled sources
www.fsc.org Cert no. SW-COC-002358
© 1996 Forest Stewardship Council

This book is dedicated to everyone who has helped develop, maintain, improve, care for, nurture, train or compete a dog from The Line.

Special thanks to Mike Ahlgren, Mike Chalupsky, Jan Munson, Andrew Barbouche, Mike Kretsch, Tory Kretsch, John Sirek (Doggie John) and Jason Kubiszewski in the kennel operations.

Terry Holzinger, Steve Marsh, Andrew Barbouche and Joe Kleaver in training the dogs.

Dr. John Bailey and Dr. Chuck Schwantes and their staff and clinics for all their help with these dogs.

Thanks to all the competitors who have competed against us and helped build the game of tournament hunting.

The people who care for these great dogs . . . Ann Miller, Lori Herold, Paula Kelley, Lori Wohlrabe, Kath, Kristi Johnson, Bob Burdit, Shelly Miller, Terry Correll, Karen Correll, Zac and Debbie Herold, Bob Monio, Lydia Monio and Shelby Monio.

The teammates — Tim Herold, Matt Herold, Rich Boumeester, Chris Slavik, Jim Miller, Andy Miller, Andrew Barbouche, Kristi Johnson, Zac Herold, Gil Roscoe, Randy Travalia, Paul Sire.

Special thanks to my cousin Mike Urseth for all the photography and creativity in developing Menz Tournament Hunter magazine.

The help and assistance of Jack David at ECW Press and the editors of this book, Emily Schultz, Crissy Boylan, Jen Hale.

Clarice Johnson for keeping everything straight, correct and on target.

To all the people around the world who have purchased and lived with dogs from The Line over the last 25 years.

To the greatest eye for puppies on earth . . . Kath.

TABLE OF CONTENTS

INTRODUCTION

As I reflect back on 30 years of running pointing dogs in fields, forests, swamps, deserts, tournaments and trials, memories flood into my mind and images abound. I remember the two separate occasions — 20 years apart — when two of my favorite dogs struck the scent of a bird while running at full speed through a field. I can still see how their noses never moved, though their bodies spun from their momentum until they stabilized on firm points. They had pivoted on their noses, two of the most athletic points I've ever seen struck. I remember how after waiting for over ten minutes in 1981 for my first dog, Merry, to return on a retrieve, she came back with a long tail rooster. We were hunting down in Iowa in an early-season snowstorm. I was so curious about how far she had actually tracked the bird, I gave up the hunt and followed the pheasant track and hers for over a mile and a half, seeing where at times the pheasant held up, thinking he had lost her, and finally the spot where she cornered him and ended it all. I was so proud of her I could barely speak, but since I was alone it didn't matter much anyway. Then within 25 yards of where she captured the 23-incher, she struck point again and a pair of roosters rose to meet my double barrel. The hunt was now finished, my three birds bagged. The cripple had led us to their hideaway.

I believe it's fair to expect that your pointing dog should point naturally; in other words, you shouldn't have to train them to do so. I think they should retrieve, if not "to hand," very close to it, and that if you want them "to hand," this skill should come within weeks of training, not months.

I think it's fair to expect them to want to hunt, to be excited when they see you with your gun. They shouldn't be afraid of water and they should be willing to swim. They should tolerate reasonably cold weather and operate in the heat up to 85 degrees Fahrenheit; then you should back off on them. Whether they have a naturally cold or hot nose, you should fairly expect them to adjust their style from ground scent to air scent on their own. I think you should accept the fact that they will fight raccoons, skunks and opossums, and if they don't, then count yourself lucky. I believe that they should be easily housebroken, but as they reach 12 or older, you should expect some accidents. When they do happen, remember all the mistakes you've made over the years and forgive them. And watch for the time when it becomes obvious that they're uncomfortable.

I believe that they'll jump up sometimes, sneak onto furniture and even slip into your bed (especially if you're on a road trip and it's a motel). I believe you should expect your females to hunt at least two hard days in a row and your males at least three. If they don't, you have yourself to blame because you've not conditioned them enough. I think you should expect your young dogs to fetch your bobbers when you take them fishing and to tangle your line in the process, but after all, dogs just ain't for fishin' anyway. I think you should expect that your dog learned nothing from the last porcupine fight, the last skunking or the previous coon encounter, even if they were quilled, sprayed or torn up. I think you should understand that they're disappointed or even angry if you leave them behind, especially if you're hunting and are bringing other dogs instead. For you to be angry as they bark and bark while you go off into the field without them is unfair. I think that your pointer will eat all the table scraps that you, your family and your friends will feed them, but that doesn't mean I think you should give them any. They don't need them and I've rarely seen a dog improved by scraps. I think you should expect your pointer to be loyal, athletic and "birdy"; the more you encourage each of these attributes, the more likely it will be that they'll hold them.

I believe that things your dog does will provoke feelings in your solar plexus that are as primal as any you might experience. They will astound you, make you proud, make you laugh and occasionally make you angry. These dogs will frighten you with their risk taking, like the time my young pup Reggie jumped off an 18-foot-high bunker and barely cleared a huge cement loading dock below — an act that could have killed him. I was terrified, but he just landed, shook himself and carried on with his life as if it were an everyday occurrence. When two of my favorites, Cent and Jäger, were gone all night, I left my jacket in the field hoping they'd find it and be there in the morning. I left food, water, the jacket

3

and a part of me when I drove away that night. When I returned in the pre-dawn morning and saw those four eyes shining off my headlights, I was too happy to be mad, too mad to be happy and so relieved that I had gotten up at 4:00 a.m. to stop my agonizing. We all just rolled around on the wet grass together — no words were needed.

When Cent got coonhound paralysis and was unable to move from the neck down for over two months, when Jäger took 23 pellets in her head and lost an eye, when Mixx got a fungal infection and was at death's door, when Bernie developed renal failure at 14 months, when Haley was hit by a car, when Abby was stolen — in each of these situations, my emotions were more attuned than they would have been during a big business deal, from watching a tear-jerker or reading a good book. This is something real happening to someone you love, who has shared some of your most cherished moments, who has seen you at your best and worst and who has given you some of their best in the process.

Many times, when people ask me, "What can I expect from a good pointing dog?" I feel that the answer they want would go something like this: "Twelve or thirteen years of finding and retrieving birds and a good companion." But I know there's so much more involved — both good and bad.

Sometimes there will be points that will take your breath away, retrieves that will amaze you, effort that will inspire pride, persistence that will make you smile, situations that will make you laugh out loud. You can expect some chewed-up stuff, a little devilry and some stubbornness, a lot of cooperation, selflessness, determination and effort. You will see beauty whether your dog is beautiful or not. Eventually there will be some gray in the muzzle, a slowing of speed and some creaky joints and then maybe some marks on the carpet from the occasional accident. At that point you'll also see the way they are and the way they were, sometimes within the same day. They'll appear to change before your eyes.

MOM, CAN I HAVE A DOG?

When it comes to dog lovers, there are two different kinds. The first just loves dogs and the second loves what dogs can do. I'm the latter.

I was only five when I started in. "Mommy, can I have a dog?" At least daily I would inquire in case something had changed. The answer would always be a firm, unequivocal "no." Rarely was there an explanation, never an apology, seldom an excuse — just a clear, concise, impossibly simple, single syllable that would be understood by people around the globe, whether their first language was English or not. "No" is close enough to the Spanish "no," the French "non," the German "nein," the Russian "nyet," the Italian "no," or the Korean "a-ni-yo" to be unmistakable. Given the fact that English today is the most common second language on the planet and that "yes" and "no" are taught at the most elementary level, it's quite likely my mother was using the single most understood word in the world. Undeterred, I would seek the next opportunity to present my case.

"Mom, do you know that this kid in Bemidji fell down a well?" I would begin.

"No, Chief, I didn't know that," she'd say.

"Well, he did and he was in that well for a day and a half and then he heard his dog barking and he yelled at the dog, 'Lady! Lady!' he yelled and the dog knew he was there and kept barking. Finally people heard the dog and found the boy who fell in the well and saved him. You know, Ma, I don't think he would have ever been found if it weren't for that dog. Do you, Mom?"

"No."

I thought hard about my failed approach and it occurred to me that I was just asking the question wrong. Of course, my little mind thought. It was the way you asked the question; the answer was "no" — without the dog the little boy wouldn't have been found. She wasn't saying no to me having a dog, she was just answering my question. My little mind rebounded immediately.

"Uh, Mom?" I asked.

"Yes?"

"I just heard on the radio about some new research that says people with pets are happier than people without them. Did you know that?"

"No," she said as she headed to the backyard to check on her laundry. I realized that I had just made the same mistake; I kept asking the question wrong. At this stage, I couldn't really read or write, but I could think, so I began to plot how to overcome my language problem.

That night, unable to sleep, I formulated questions in my mind. "Mom, wouldn't you like to have a happy, secure, responsible son who would clean up the crap and never get lost because he fell in a well?" As I tossed, I realized this was a perfect question because she'd have to say yes. She certainly loved me and wouldn't want me to be unhappy, insecure, irresponsible, unwilling to clean up crap or lost down a well. Shortly after this breakthrough struck me, I fell contentedly to sleep.

In the morning I arose and went down to breakfast. My father, Big Al, had already gone to work. He was a mail carrier and got up two hours earlier than the rest of us. Mom was strictly coffee and toast; I piled into my cereal and had some toast, too. My sister would eat Kix and pour sugar all over them, which I never understood. Just as I was about to spring my perfect sentence, the phone rang and my mother answered it. My sister and I ate while my mother chatted with my cousin Jean. She was my babysitter, cousin and pal. She was really lucky 'cause she was very pretty, had a boyfriend and, most of all, had a dog named Buttons — kind of a collie and setter cross. To most, he might have been a mutt, but to me, when I was dreaming of hunting, he would become a huntin' setter that would run with the big dogs across fields filled with pheasant. Or, if my mental adventures were more urban, Buttons could sniff clothes and find lost kids or solve small crimes in my imaginary world. Whatever Buttons did or didn't do wasn't important; I knew I loved him and whenever I'd go to Jean's house, he would greet me, stay by me, protect me, play ball with me and sit under the table to make sure my green beans got eaten, which was important, because I couldn't get my dessert until they were gone.

By the time she got off the phone with Jean, it was time for my Mom to go, so my perfect question would have to wait.

That night after supper the situation seemed ideal. I offered to dry the dishes. Mom was a little surprised, but she accepted my offer. The radio was on and as if on cue, the song that came on was "How Much Is That Doggie in the Window?" Not wanting to seem too opportunistic, I waited until it was over, and then as the music faded I asked "the question." I never knew how hard it could be to talk to your mother about something so important.

"You know, Mom, if you got lost and fell in a well of crap, I'd be happy, secure and responsible. Don't you?"

She looked at me with the oddest look. As I was realizing how badly I had screwed up my perfectly framed question, she lunged.

I never knew that little woman could move so fast. She had me by the arm and into a half nelson, my head was over the sink and, before I could say one more convoluted word, my mouth was full of dish soap and bubbling ferociously.

"Where did you learn to talk like that? Did you learn that from that Larry Sollie?"

Thank goodness I'd already eaten supper or I would have gone to bed hungry. As I lay there that night I didn't know how I could have screwed it up so bad. How did "Mom, wouldn't you like to have a happy, secure, responsible son who would clean up the crap and never get lost because he fell in a well?" lead to a me being sent to bed early with the taste of soap in my mouth? And I never even had the chance to ask for my dog. I'm convinced to this day that if I had properly executed "the question" that night, she would have said yes. As it was, I continued to try constantly until I turned 14, and I still tried occasionally after.

Being a mail carrier, my dad would find stray dogs all the time and he sometimes brought them home. He was kind of the unofficial dogcatcher in the neighborhood. There was a "Three-Day Rule." My mother would allow a dog around for three days, no longer. In those three days, my job was to find where the dog belonged. The emotions this conjured were deeply conflicting as I would reunite the dogs I coveted with their owners, receiving everything from tips to threats in exchange.

Rex was a lovable little half-Lab who never broke the Three-Day Rule, though he stayed with us on four or five separate occasions. He would pull wagons in our little sidewalk parades and guarded lemonade stands from trouble. When Rex's family moved, it put a permanent end to his visits.

COUSINS

My cousin Jean had a younger sister named Mar. She was 16 and a lot of fun, too. She used to help take care of me as well. We always had a ball together. Living in Minnesota we had great winters where we could ice skate, slide and toboggan. The two were young enough to enjoy doing these things. I remember the time we went to Longfellow Library by Minnehaha Creek where there was a great toboggan hill. The snow was perfect and we tobogganed down the normal route for several runs, and then the girls decided we should take the forest run and dodge the trees. To me this sounded like the best idea ever. It was almost as good as spending a month with Rin Tin Tin. The three of us packed onto the toboggan and began the forest run. We dodged tree number one, skirted by tree number two, skinned past tree number three and brushed up against tree number four, careening down the steep hill. It was tree number five that changed our momentum. We hit it dead on and I flew like a mortar round out of the toboggan. The girls rolled out to each side, moaning. The toboggan was chipped and cracked down the center. I lay in a snow bank and the snow around my head was getting redder and redder. When the girls reached me, their silence was more frightening than if they had been screaming. They looked down at me and slowly shook their heads back and forth. Almost in unison they said, "Aunt Bee is gonna kill us!"

My mother was only five feet tall and 110 pounds, but she was known to be tough, firm and feisty. She could, with a quick glance, communicate more than most people could with a hundred words. You knew from her eyes if she was happy, sad, angry, empathetic, furious, concerned, worried, anxious or most anything. She didn't talk a lot, there was no need. She had other ways to communicate that could be intimidating.

The blood was pouring from my nose and lip. The girls moved close to me now and began to hug me.

"You okay, Chief? Are you okay? Wow, that's quite a cut!" Mar said. At this point, I'd never been cut before, to the best of my memory. I started to whimper about my condition and Mar said, "Don't worry, Chief, you'll be okay, you'll be okay," at which point I heard Jean say, "Don't promise too much, Mar, he's a mess," which did nothing to slow my tears. With handkerchiefs they began to stop my bleeding, using snow to help, and within minutes I was recovering, the bleeding was slowed and then they did an inventory on my bones and joints to see if they were broken or damaged. When the results were in, I had a split lip and an old-fashioned bloody nose. We walked the six blocks back to their house as if we were Napoleon retreating from Moscow. We walked slowly, the girls pulling me on the toboggan behind them.

I was bloody, but feeling pretty good, and while I wouldn't have suggested another try at the "forest run," I was doing okay. When we got to the house, Buttons was there and very curious about my injuries, but the girls whooshed him away while they cleaned me up. The whole way back I could hear them saying, "Bee is gonna kill us. We just about killed Chief," and then they'd make faces as to how they thought my mother might react. Even at my age I knew she could hurt you more with a look than anything else.

It would be at least three hours before my mother would show up and I was making a miraculous recovery. Except for the swollen face and the cut lip, I was as good as new, so my mind returned to its most fervent subject: how could I get a dog? Assessing the situation, I realized that the accident must have been pretty bad to scare Jean and Mar the way it did and that they were really concerned and sympathetic when they first saw me. So I thought, "Mom will be sympathetic, too, when she sees me," and the window opened.

The girls had tucked me into bed, left some ice for my lip and had me take a nap. Tired as I was, I couldn't sleep while thinking of the opportunity before me. I crawled out of bed and found in the closet some old crutches, a cane, some Ace bandages and tape that belonged to my Uncle George. I already had some gauze and mercurochrome, so I went to work. I put the cane and crutches by the bed and nightstand, wrapped my legs with Ace bandages, put gauze around my arms and forehead and touched it up with the mer-curochrome, which looked like blood to me. Then I waited for my mother who would certainly be the most sympathetic I'd ever seen her.

I could hear the girls whispering in the hallway, but I couldn't hear everything. "Chief was hurt. . . . We didn't mean to. . . . He's resting. . . . We didn't think he needed an ambulance. . . ." were some of the things I made out. My mother never said a word, she just listened. Then the door opened a little and I could see the three of them peeking through the crack. My mother's head was the lowest, Mar next, Jean on top. They just stared at me, my bandages, the gauze, the mercurochrome, the crutches, the cane. I could see through my half-open eyes the surprise on the girls' faces.

My mother stepped forward alone, the girls stayed by the door. As I pretended to sleep, I anticipated her maternal concern. She slowly came forward and leaned over the bed.

"Chief, wake up," she whispered.

I didn't move. As I was lying there she picked up the crutch I had placed by the bed. As she raised it, she must have seen that it was way too high for her, much less me.

"Billy, wake up," she said a little more loudly.

I shook my head groggily, to communicate my disorientation. She smiled.

"How are you, Chief?" she asked gently.

I shook my head as if to say "Not too good, Mom."

"Now sit up and let me look at you," she continued, which I tried to do, but feigned weakness.

The girls were still watching from the door, more alarmed now than before, confused by my new injuries. Finally, she did it. Mom finally asked the question I'd been waiting for.

"Is there anything I can do for you?" The ultimate question, she had let her guard down and opened the gates. Even her eyes held that sympathetic gaze that comes with parental guilt. After all, I did get hurt on her watch. Jean and Mar peered on and then I said it.

"Mom, I think I'd feel a whole lot better if I had a puppy."

It was as if an artillery round had been dropped into the room. My mother quickly straightened up, the girls in sync said "Why, that little faker!" My mother grabbed that crutch and lifted it over her head as if to smash it down on the portion of the bed that my legs inhabited. With a quickness I didn't know I possessed, I swung my legs out of the way. The girls came rushing into the room.

"Why you little rat," Jean yelled. "Faker! I'm gonna give you another fat lip," Mar said.

I was curled upright in the far corner of the bed, against the wall, with my three favorite women yelling and threatening me, one brandishing a weapon. Finally, I said, "Well, you gotta admit I sure could use a dog about now to get me out of this mess!"

Mom had never even said "no," but the subject was decisively closed.

PHYLLIS

It was a small festival at our local YMCA. There was a cakewalk, turtle races, skill games and a small carnival. Usually my dad would have gone with me to something like this, but as it was close to Christmas, the mail carriers needed to work on Saturdays. I went to the carnival with Bob Peterson, my dad's friend and the guy who years later taught me to hunt. I was nine at the time. By now everybody knew that I wanted a dog, but they also knew my mother's unalterable position. As the carnival was wrapping up, my eye was drawn to eight six-foot-long tracks where mice would race from one end to the other. I watched the last five races and then people started packing things up. The carnival was over.

I hadn't really thought twice about the fate of

the mice once the festival ended, but much to my surprise, Bob Peterson and Irv Bracker had conspired that, since I was such a pet lover, I should go home with one of these avid competitors. The mouse I got was even purported to be the winningest mouse on the track. For all I knew, it was a famous mouse and might be written about in tomorrow morning's paper. They gave the mouse to me in such a way I couldn't say no, even if I wanted to, which I didn't.

By the time I got home I had named the mouse Phyllis, which was Bob's wife's name, and I was actually growing fond of the little rodent that was now living in a Chinese food take-out container. As I entered the door to my house, I realized this was not something to keep secret; it was the first animal I had ever gotten. It had been "awarded" to me by Bob Peterson and Irv Bracker. I had concluded it was in recognition of meritorious behavior that day. After all, there were over 100 youngsters at the carnival to whom they could have given the mouse, including their own sons, but they chose me. My mind had not focused on whether this might have been a gag, of which my parents were the victims. No, this was all about me.

"Mom, look what I was awarded!" I yelled as I came in the door. Expecting a prize, medal, ribbon, trophy, plaque, certificate or something equally inanimate, you can imagine her surprise when she saw a Chinese take-out container. Thinking the best, she said, "Chow Mein?"

"No, no, Mom, much more important than that — it's a mouse!" With those eyes that could communicate so much, she squinted — she exhibited no fear, no anxiety, she just looked perplexed.

"Who awarded this to you?" she asked, cutting to the quick.

"Bob and Irv," I shot back.

"For what, exactly?"

"I think it was for my meritorious behavior, Mom, but they didn't want to print that on here, you know."

Now one of her eyes went up and the other stayed in place. Her nose wrinkled and her right lip moved up. Not wanting to destabilize her only son, she said, "Well congratulations. I'll get a shoe box."

We made a nest out of paper and grass, put some water in a little muffin cup and made holes in the top of the shoe box. By this time almost nobody called me Chief anymore, so on the box I wrote "For Meritorious Behavior from the YMCA to Billy U." I then went outside to play.

An hour later when I came in to check on Phyllis (my award for meritorious behavior), I was aghast to find that there was a hole in the side of the box where she had chewed right through the 'E,' 'R' and 'I,' causing the reader at a quick glance to see a portion of the 'M,' which now looked like an 'N,' then the hole, followed by "torious." The box now appeared to read "notorious," but more importantly — Phyllis was on the loose. There's no easy way to tell your mother that your pet mouse is loose in the house, especially when it's as prized as Phyllis. I simply brought her the box and showed her. Now my mother didn't swear as a matter of practice. She had her own expressions: "jumpin' Jehosaphat" and "for crying out loud" were a couple of them, but not strong enough for this. "Judas Priest" wouldn't suffice either. As always, her eyes were the best communicators and they said, "Holy shit, I better get that damned mouse and then I'm gonna get that damned Peterson."

She and I searched the house and we found Phyllis in the

couch, between the cushions, already chewing away at the fabric.

"Mom, do you think we need a new trophy case for my award?" I asked. I knew I was pushing it a little bit, but by this time I had gotten pretty good at developing lines that at least had a chance.

"When your father gets home, he'll help," was what her lips said, while her eyes said, "Phyllis ain't dead yet."

Dad got the best and strongest dovetailed 25-cigar box I'd ever seen. The wood looked like mahogany and the little metal clasp was a perfect lock. He and I moved the nest and the water into Phyllis' new home and I threw the "notorious" shoe box away. My sister got home and we enjoyed an uneventful supper as the four of us had pot roast, which my dad, Big Al, excelled at preparing. He was the cook in our family and was really good at it. Mom seemed preoccupied, and after supper she told dad she was going to the pet store. My ears physically raised, my mouth moved as if possessed. "Pet store," my lips mimed. I waited with the highest anticipation, as she was gone about an hour. When she pulled up, I was in my bedroom with my periscope, which could see over my window sill and down to the garage. I was sitting on the floor, unseen, spying through the periscope as to the outcome of the pet store visit. When I saw her, she had three small containers. There was no quick-reflexed beagle or long-legged greyhound. There was no red-and-white Brittany or lumbering Saint Bernard — just three small boxes. My disappointment was total.

They said it was time to say good night to Phyllis, so dutifully I went downstairs to do it. Well, I would have bet you 40 cat's eyes and a dozen steelies, 10 shooters and 50 clearies that the mouse couldn't have eaten through that fake mahogany cigar box, but if I had made such a bet, I would have lost all my valuable marbles. There was no doubt about it — Phyllis was gone and my new trophy case had a hole in it.

"Mom, Mom," I yelled. "Phyllis has left the trophy case, Phyllis has left the trophy case!"

Once again she spoke not. She was upstairs, so I couldn't see her eyes, but suddenly I heard a reflex reaction that people have had to mice for millennia. She just screamed, like Janet Leigh in *Psycho*. I think her frustrations had added up. By the time she got downstairs, she was cool again and we started our hunt. We searched the laundry basket, the old newspapers, the old magazines, all the stored boxes in the pantry and finally we grabbed Phyllis in the paint rags. She spent the night in an old coffee can, inside a 50-gallon garbage can, in solitary confinement, in the high-security, lockdown unit. None of us needed any more jailbreaks.

The next morning Mom showed me the pet store purchases. As she did, she said, "You know, Billy, Phyllis will be happiest in the wild. She keeps breaking out because she wants to be in the outdoors. You don't feel good about that maximum-security unit you've created, do you?"

"No," I responded.

"Do you agree we should take her to Mother's Lake?"

"Yeah, I agree it'll be best."

She then showed me the three turtles she had bought as gifts for the three Peterson boys at the pet shop.

"Wow, they get turtles?" I asked. "Are they ever lucky!"

"What'll be even more fun is that they and Bob can go to the pet store and pick out an aquarium, rocks, sand, liners, bridges, houses, water troughs, turtle toys, turtle food and all kinds of other things. Aren't they lucky?" she smiled.

"Oh yeah," I said. Later I heard Bob say that "all that turtle crap cost me over $30 at the pet store. That damn mouse sure got expensive." And these were 1958 dollars.

We went together to Mother's Lake to release Phyllis. My mom chose the area, I chose the spot. I wanted her to have good grasses, and there was an old chicken coop nearby that I knew would be good shelter. There was water, even though mice don't need much. I walked around until I saw another mouse and knew that she'd have company. Before I released her, I looked at my mom and said, "Mom, don't you think we could take a mouse this important and trade her in at the pet store for a dog?" She never said a word; her eyes told me everything. "No" was the unspoken, one-syllable word. I released Phyllis and she ran in the direction I had seen the other mouse go.

BUDDY AND THE FARM

Starting at age 11, I would pack up and move for most of the summer to my godparents' farm in Heron Lake, Minnesota. This created a chance for me to get out of the city and to learn how country kids lived. It was a farm with dairy cows, beef cattle, pigs and chickens; they grew corn, soy beans, alfalfa, flax and did custom work for other farmers. They also owned horses and, most important for me, they had a dog — Buddy.

My jobs on the farm were to help milk the cows in the morning, let them out to pasture, do field work, check fences, haul wagons, get the cows in for the afternoon milking, milk the cows again and then I'd usually be done for the day. Buddy followed me everywhere; he'd be with me during both milkings, ride with me if I drove a truck, run beside me if I was on the tractor, walk out with me to get the cows and then milk with me some more. We were inseparable.

The farm had about six boys working on it, and they ranged from sons to future sons-in-law to hired hands to neighbors, but no matter how you cut it, Uncle Art was the Big Boss and I was at the bottom of the pecking order. The other boys were 16, 17, even 18 years old. They were country kids, not city boys, and with the age differences, I was the butt of every joke, the victim of every prank and the rookie in every situation. There was only one living thing who thought I was something and that was Buddy. He accepted me the way dogs do: what ya see is what ya get; you be good to me, I'll be good to you.

Now make no mistake about it, some of the hazing I took was well deserved, like the time I was hauling wagons in from the field. I was feeling pretty powerful driving that tractor. With the smell of diesel exhaust filling my nose and the fresh breeze hitting my face, I'd haul the empty wagons out to the field and bring the full ones back to the farm's elevator to be unloaded. As I'd go, Buddy would run alongside. On this particular afternoon I had made a good ten trips or so and only had another one or two left before Buddy and I had to start bringing the cows in for milking. I backed up carefully to the full wagon, and, not being familiar with this one, I hooked it up to the tractor, but absentmindedly used the tongue extension to pin the tongue onto the tractor. The effect was that I pulled away with only the steel tongue of the wagon behind me and completely left the wagon in the field. As I pulled away, Buddy just stood there and didn't run after me like always. I quickly turned and yelled, "Come on, Buddy," but never noticed, even when I looked back, that I wasn't pulling the wagon. When I got to the gravel, Old Farmer Kiffmeier sidled up next to me, snickering and pointing to the back of my tractor. I just waved and smiled. When I got to the blacktop, someone else came by and honked. I could hear some laughing and somebody said, "That's the city kid," but I was none the wiser. As I pulled into the farmyard, it was just my luck that it was afternoon lunch time, so a lot of the girls and even some of the boys were around the house. They pointed and laughed. I just waved as I confidently pulled my false cargo to its destination. It wasn't until I got off the tractor to unhitch my load that I realized what I had done. Uncle Art simply said, "Well, Chief, it won't take long to unload this one." Buddy was loyal enough to follow me all the way back out to the field. As we drove by the farmhouse, the hooting and hollering was pretty loud and even the sound of an Oliver tractor couldn't drown out the laughter.

I really wanted to learn how to ride a horse while I was on the farm. I was brought up on Westerns — *The Roy Rogers Show*, *Hopalong Cassidy Hour*, *Gunsmoke*, *Bonanza* and *Have Gun Will Travel* were all standard fare. Every time I had a chance I'd ask the big boys, "Will you teach me to ride, will you teach me to ride?" I was thinking how cool it would be if I could ride out to get the cows on horseback with Buddy running right along for the round-up each afternoon. One day we were at dinner and all the big boys were there, and I asked Aunt Jeanette if she thought I should learn to ride. All the big boys laughed, and then she said with a lot of sympathy for me, the little goat, "I think it would be a good idea." The big boys went quiet 'cause she had a lot of sway, so I had the feeling that those big boys were under orders to teach me to ride. I was elated and told Buddy about the recent developments. I don't think he understood, but I think he sensed my excitement.

A couple of days later my riding career was held up because as I pulled a tractor up to a fuel tank, I had managed to drive the tractor's front tire over the fuel hose. I then tore the nozzle off the hose, resulting in gallons and gallons of fuel spilling all over the ground. It was a good thing I wasn't experimenting with cigarettes at the time, like some of the other boys.

It took me a good hour to get the hose back on the tank and get things somewhat back to normal. About then Uncle Art showed up and asked me what was going on. As he was tapping his pipe onto the ground, I told him my story. I never knew that Uncle Art could dance as well as he could. With no music at all he started jumping around, kicking ashes, sparks, dirt and muddy gasoline, thinking he may have just cleaned his last pipe. I helped the best I could, but I had the feeling I had probably done quite a bit already. That man rarely swore and he certainly didn't use the words that he used on that occasion very often at all, but on that day and under those circumstances, he made an execption. Buddy maintained his distance and only started hanging around with me again after I no longer smelled like gas.

The big boys announced at breakfast that I would get my first riding lesson that night. I felt like it was my birthday. Alan said, "Yep, tonight will be Chief's first lesson. He'll use my horse, the Palomino Lancelot, and we'll do it right after milk-ing and before supper." Now eating on the farm involved its own vocabulary. You ate two breakfasts: one before morning chores (cereal, fruit, juice, toast) at about 6:00 a.m. and then the second breakfast (bacon, eggs, pancakes, French toast) when chores and milking were over, at about 8:00 a.m. There were two lunches, not to be confused with dinner. At noon came dinner, which was the biggest meal of the day (meat, potatoes, vegetables, bread, dessert). It was delicious. The first lunch was probably in the field about 10:30 a.m. with sandwiches, fruit and Kool-Aid. The second lunch was at about 2:30 p.m. or so with more sandwiches, cookies, cake and Kool-Aid. After evening chores and milking, came supper. We worked hard and were hungry for every meal. Suppers were lighter than dinner, but still substantial (hamburgers, sausages, salads, desserts). My riding lesson was right before supper and after evening chores.

"Wow, Roy, I'm gonna learn to ride tonight."

Roy said, "You know, kid, you're gonna need a lesson every night for a week. You're not going to learn to ride in one night."

That sobered me up, but then I realized of course that he was right and this was going to be a process.

Buddy and I rushed through chores, spilling more milk than usual. Buddy was pleased, but I was glad Uncle Art hadn't caught me. My screw-ups were too numerous. The decision was made that my riding lesson was to take place in the steer lot. This was about the size of a hockey rink and it held about 80 steers who were good at putting it in one end and letting it come out the other. The manure was about two to three feet deep. Alan brought out Lancelot as Buddy and I arrived. He had on a really old saddle I had never seen before, but he looked beautiful. At the center of the steer lot, he held Lancelot and called for me to approach the horse. All the big boys were there. They all finished work early to see my riding lesson. They sat on the fence, most of them with cigarettes and big smiles. These guys had never cared so much about me before. I concluded they just must love horses, too.

Alan carefully showed me how to mount from the left side which I did and now I was up on my first real horse. This was no pony!

"Now, if you want to be a great rider . . ." Alan said.

"I do," I interrupted.

". . . then you've got to learn the most important part of riding." He stopped talking for at least ten seconds, at which point I asked, "Which is?"

"Falling," he replied. "Now fall off to the left," which I did. "Remount," which I did. "Fall to the right," which I did. "Remount."

The big boys were howling. They were laughing like they were at a Bob Hope show. With each fall I was more and more covered with steer manure. "Remount. Roll off the back," which I did. "Remount. Forward roll to the left," which I did. Then the dinner bell rang and every big boy ran for the supper table, laughing and back-slapping as they went. Alan stopped, turned and said, "Get the horse unsaddled and put away and clean yourself off. Art ain't gonna have you at the dinner table looking and smelling like that."

My first riding lesson had gone well, I thought. I had learned to fall off a horse six or seven different ways. I hadn't gotten hurt and had no fear of falling at all at this point. I went over and unsaddled Lancelot, then went to the well hydrant and washed up. I realized then, as even Buddy kept his distance, that I'd have to change clothes completely after an icy hydrant hosing before I got to supper.

When I walked into supper the boys started laughing again for the fifth or sixth time that evening. They were having trouble breathing. Some of them were wiping tears out of their eyes. As I surveyed the table, I realized that they had eaten every scrap of food. Luckily, so did Aunt Jeannette. As they filed out to have their cigarettes, she made a special little supper just for me. When I finished it, Buddy and I played catch.

I would never again be afraid of riding or falling off a horse. I rode the rest of that summer and every chance I've had for most of my life.

THE LOST DOG

When he arrived there was a special energy — his tail wagged faster than other dogs, his eyes were more alive, his mind more alert. He was quicker to fetch the ball and very observant of the threshold of our house. He was a black Lab and one of the many strays my dad, the mail carrier, brought home. I knew the drill: find the owners and get him home.

By now I knew that most of the lost dogs my dad found were from more than six but less than 12 blocks from our house, so that created a search zone within which to work. With the airport six blocks to the south and Lake Nokomis six blocks to the west, most of the lost dogs were from the north and east. I was now old enough to bicycle all through the neighborhood, and this Lab looked like he'd be easy to repatriate because he was clearly a dog that people had trained and cared about. He was only two or three years old and had every trait that attracts people to dogs — good conformation, pleasant disposition, obedient, biddable. He was a two-speed dog, docile and mellow when he should be and a spitfire when he could be. I had read about dogs like this in books and it was a trait that the British writers greatly admired, but one that Americans didn't seem to recognize at that time.

I pedaled, put up posters, talked to other kids and adults. Big Al would do the same as he covered the neighborhood on his parcel post route. I'll never know why and I never asked, but as I came home that evening with no leads, I saw my mother and the dog in the backyard. She was playing with him and giving him single pieces of Dog Chow as treats. They were actually playing! I knew I shouldn't let my hopes soar, but they certainly did.

"No leads, Ma!" I yelled as I put the bike down. She had stopped playing with the dog and walked toward me.

"Maybe tomorrow," she said.

When Dad came home from work he had the same results.

"Nobody seems to know him," Big Al offered.

"He's definitely somebody's dog, Dad. Even his nails are trimmed. He's got lots of training. I think somebody probably even paid money for this dog. He's not a mix, he's purebred Labrador," I said.

"But why no license, no collar?" Big Al asked.

"I just don't know, I just don't know." I shook my head as I talked.

The Lab and I played fetch until supper. I'd throw the ball as far as I could and he'd run it down in no time, rushing back to me. He would sit on my left side and hold the ball in his mouth until I said "give," at which time he'd drop it in my hand. At supper we all talked about the mysterious Lab. My sister Bonnie had fallen for him, too. Two years younger than me, she wanted a dog as badly as I did.

"What else have you learned about him, Bill?" my dad asked.

"Well, he's a 'here' dog, not a 'come' dog. Most professional dog trainers use 'here' and most amateurs say 'come.' He drops on 'give,' not on 'drop' or 'release.' He sits on command, downs on command, doesn't roll over or beg. He's not into circus tricks or cute stuff. He's in good condition, not fat, not thin, and could run all day. He trusts people. When I raised my hand as if I was going to hit him, he didn't shy, not at all. Whoever has had him has been good to him," I concluded.

Then my sister piped up. "We need to figure out his name."

"Why don't we just ask him?" I smart-alecked back to her.

"Okay, I will!" she said and left the table.

In short order little Bonnie had the dog on the back porch and she had the dog lying down. At that point she began to say dog names, not as commands, but as words in a normal voice.

"Max, Alex, Bullet, Tom, Ben." She was listing dozens. It was then I realized that she had a pretty good idea and I joined her on the porch. We took turns. The Lab lay there as we said names.

"Rocky, Moochy, Rex, Bolt, Ranger, Sam, Bear, Buddy, Casey, Fido, Chip, Gus, Hobo, Tank."

Then suddenly it was my turn and I said "Duke." On

hearing the name the Lab jumped up and wagged his tail. The two of us started to bounce up and down.

"Duke, Duke, Duke," we yelled. "Mom, it's Duke! Dad, it's Duke!"

They both came outside and in minutes we could prove his name was Duke.

"Duke, here." "Duke, come here." "Duke, sit." "Duke, fetch."

It all proved out. I thought I knew everything about dogs, but it was my little sister that figured out how to have him tell us his name. Now our signs could be more specific — and the search continued.

At the end of the third day we all knew that the Three-Day Rule was in effect. My mother never brought it up, my father never reminded us. We just knew that the clock was ticking. We had never been in this spot before because we had never not found the owners in three days. The implication of the Three-Day Rule was that he couldn't stay at our house more than three days and we thought that meant the dog pound. At that time I believed that if we couldn't find the owners, the dog pound never would, and I couldn't think about what would happen to Duke. All through supper nobody brought up the Three-Day Rule. There was just nervous chatter to make sure there were no lulls in the conversation; all of us did it.

After supper I went out to play with Duke, and at about 8:00 p.m. heavy clouds were coming from the west. It was obvious it was going to rain. Up until now he'd just slept outside in an old clothes basket with a blanket on the bottom. When it began to rain about 9:00 p.m., I went in and Mom said, "Is it raining yet?"

"Yeah, it just started," I said.

"Bring Duke in, Billy," she said. Then I looked in the corner of the kitchen and there was wooden box with a red blanket. It was a bed for Duke! Mom had put it there!

I didn't say a word and just called Duke in. He came very reluctantly.

"He doesn't go in the living room, Bill," she said clearly. In the next half hour he knew the line of demarcation: kitchen "yes," living room "no." He curled up in his box and slept fitfully through the storm. By 6:30 the next morning both my sister and I were by his box, ready to play.

Both Dad and I redoubled our efforts to find Duke's owners, but at the end of a week we had found nothing. Our searches found nobody; our signs drew no phone calls. We all avoided direct discussion of the topic.

I never asked, "Can we keep him?" My sister never said, "Does that mean Duke is ours?" My dad never said, "What do you think, Bee, can we keep him?" My mom never said, "We're over the Three-Day Rule" or "It's time for him to go." We moved from strained silence to nervous chatter to avoid the topic. Duke and I would play catch every day, then we'd head to Lake Nokomis where he would swim after tennis balls I'd launch into the lake. We'd walk up to Mother's Lake where I had released Phyllis five years earlier, and Duke would flush pheasants from the switch grass and cattails. I had never been so happy. We were all happy.

My dad always encouraged me to write and it seemed obvious that I should write an ad to find Duke's owners, though I didn't know what it might cost to run such an ad in the Minneapolis paper. Economy wasn't my concern, results were.

The ad read:

We've found Duke! Black Lab, 2-3 years old. Responds to "here," "give," "down." Retrieves all day, finds pheasants, doesn't do silly circus tricks. A two-speed dog. We've taken good care of him. Call 724-3421.

We would spend every day together. I'd bike, he'd run next to me. There were no leash laws in those days. If I went fishing, he'd go fishing. If I'd go to the park, he'd go to the park and he could be the center of attention or fade into the scenery. He was welcome everywhere. If I wasn't with him, my sister was. There was no talk about the Three-Day Rule. He slept in the kitchen and never went in the living room. It seems that during the Cold War people became used to unspoken dilemmas. There was the 38th Parallel in Korea, the 17th Parallel in Vietnam, the Berlin Corridor. They all just existed and people didn't push to erase them; they just lived within the status quo.

It was the end of the second week on a Saturday that the phone rang. I could hear my mother answer. Her voice didn't reveal the ominous nature of the call. "Yes," she said, "this is 724-3421. Yes, we ran the ad. Yes, the dog is here. We're down by Lake Nokomis. Yes, you can come by around four o'clock. That's 5417 — 28th Avenue."

She couldn't look at me. She stood by the kitchen window for five minutes and didn't turn her head. At age 11 I was too old to cry, but I did anyway. At nine my sister wasn't too old to cry, and she did. At 53 my dad was way too old to cry, but he shed some tears, too.

I spent the rest of the morning and the entire afternoon

with Duke. We did all the things we loved to do. My sister was with us sometimes, too, but she kept tearing up. At about 3:30 p.m. my dad said, "Let's talk."

We sat down at the picnic table and he said, "You did the right thing with that ad, you know that don't you?" I nodded, but I didn't want to talk.

When they came to pick Duke up, they had a station wagon. When Duke saw the car he got excited. I knew immediately that it was them and they were his real masters. The man was in his forties and in good shape. I knew he was a hunter just by looking at him. The boy was older than me by a couple of years. He and Duke rolled and "wrassled" on our front lawn the minute they saw each other.

"Oh, Duke," he yelled. "Oh, Duke."

The woman got out of the car, too. She smiled, then laughed as she saw them wrassling. My dad introduced himself and Duke's master did the same.

"He was in a fenced backyard," the man said. "I don't know how he could have gotten out."

"I don't either," my dad said.

"We live way up in north Minneapolis. I don't know how he got this far south," he continued. "If you hadn't run the ad, we'd have never found him. We had posters up all over the north side, but who would have guessed he'd be 15 miles away. Say, that was quite an ad you wrote. A neighbor of mine saw it and said, 'They've got your dog, Ken.' You sure know dogs. What kind do you have, Al?"

"Well, I work for the post office and we're kind of specialists at returning them," Big Al answered.

I watched the whole thing through the same kitchen window my mother had stood by for five minutes when the call first came in. I watched it through my periscope and remained unseen. I couldn't say goodbye to Duke. I couldn't say hello to the other boy. I couldn't meet the guy who had trained the dog I loved. He had done me a favor by showing me how good a dog can be, how good they can make you feel and I had done him a favor by getting his dog back to him and his family.

WHEN JEFF GOT HIS DOG

A year had gone by since Duke was repatriated. That next summer, I went to the farm in Heron Lake for one of my annual sojourns to the country. At this stage, I was making fewer gaffs and was less of a screw-up than I had been early on. I was still the city kid, but I wasn't such a rookie, and by then I really did ride Lancelot out to round up the cows. Buddy and I would go each afternoon. I was also learning to shoot and had a .22 caliber rifle that was great for shooting frogs, which I'd clean and we'd eat the legs; for hunting rabbits, which we ate after the first frost; and for hitting targets, which I practiced all the time. That was the first year that I really felt comfortable shooting and hunting, and I had gotten pretty good at it.

The hardest thing about going to the farm, as much as I liked it there, was that I would be away from my friends for about eight weeks. Tom Peterson (Bob's son) and I were good friends. We weren't in the same grade so that tended to create a distance in our relationship, especially since we were even in different schools that year. Before I went out to the farm, I had been spending more time with Jeff. When I got back, I had all kinds of adventure stories for him. I had ridden a horse almost every day. I had hunted constantly during my time off. I had learned to drive a truck with a straight stick and could mow and rake hay. I had a beer after baling hay on a hot summer day, and I could have smoked cigarettes any time I wanted. I took a chew of snuff, got dizzy, and though I almost barfed, I didn't, so I was pretty proud. Jeff had some stories, too, but they were pretty lame city-type stories that really didn't have much adventure in them. He'd tell me about riding his bike. One day he played golf, not on a golf course, but in a city park. He'd mowed lawns all summer. I mean, this was dull, but I listened politely. After an hour or so of catching up, I knew I had drawn the long straw that summer and that Jeff's life had been pretty boring.

It was September and that meant that the apples and pears at the airport would be ripe, so off we went, exploring. The airport at that time was always expanding, and as it grew, it began to wipe out the last working farms in the city. They bought up the land, they'd tear down the farmhouses, but leave the groves and orchards intact. There were a lot of fruit trees in those groves and the fruit would go to waste unless us boys showed up. We'd stuff ourselves and then bring home bags full of apples and pears and plums for our parents. Mom would bake apple crisps, pies and turnovers and Dad would make sauces. As we went, we'd scout out trails and spots for the traps that we'd be setting around Mother's Lake and on the airport land over the next few months. Jeff and I would walk through the tall grasses, mostly switch grass and wheat grass, and scare up pheasants as we went. When we got too close to the water line, we'd launch mallards and teal into the air. In the thick spots, we'd jump deer that would then run from us out onto the airport runways. There were no fences around the airport in those days.

"We're close to stove-pipe time," I told Jeff. "Those pheasants are full-grown. We can set out our stove-pipe traps anytime."

"Yeah, we can, but it would be a lot more fun to have a dog and go shootin' 'em, wouldn't it?" he asked.

Well, of course he was right, but we were in the city limits and even stove-pipe traps weren't exactly legal, but they were harmless, so no one ever said anything about them. But shooting over a bird dog — well, that would be another story. The stove-pipe trap was just a piece of stove pipe; we'd close off one end and put it on the ground with corn kernels leading into it. The pheasant would feed its way into the pipe and then be afraid to back out. Pheasants don't walk backwards. Then we'd arrive, snatch them out of the pipe and have fresh pheasant for dinner, always a treat. Jeff and I shared our harvest; we worked equally and we shared equally.

Trapping is actually a lot of work. You have to choose the locations for your traps, set the traps, stake the traps, check them every day, reset them and move the ones that aren't working. You had to kill your catch, skin it, stretch it, dry it, and then sell it. We trapped because we loved it. We enjoyed being outside, the long walks and the physicality of trapping, the getting wet, the carrying our catch over our backs all the way home. Other kids would be amazed as we walked out with muskrats, foxes, coons, pheasants and even the occasional mink. We thought we were mountain men even though there was a bus stop not four blocks from our trap line. We never took it, of course; what "real trapper" would ever be caught dead on a bus?

One day we found a bike in the tall grasses. It was in great shape; it was an English bike, as we called them in those days. We looked all around for who could have left it there.

I said, "Let's bring it in and I'll find the owner. With some signs and a few tricks we'll solve this mystery." As I looked closer, I saw that there was even a license on the bike that would make it really easy to return it.

Then Jeff said, "No, let's leave it here. Somebody probably just stashed it in the weeds and will come back for it."

"Well, okay. I kinda doubt it, though. It looks like somebody took a joy ride and dumped it here." I let it slide and we left the bike there. The next day we checked the trap line and discovered the bike was still there.

"You know what," Jeff said, "this is ours now. We gave the guy a chance, now it's ours."

"I don't want it, Jeff. I can find the guy and get it back to him."

Then I noticed that the license, the metal tape that I had seen the day before, had been scraped off.

"I wouldn't be so sure, Sherlock. There's no license on this bike."

I quietly acknowledged that the license was gone. Jeff took the bike.

"Half of it's yours!" he said. I shook my head. "No thanks."

We continued to trap and had a good year. We shared everything 50/50. We were making money because fur prices were pretty good, and pheasants and rabbits were always welcome. Big Al could cook them up really, really well.

In early December, we began to take turns checking the line — me one day, Jeff the next. It worked well because we both had more schoolwork and there was no sense in us both going every time. One day, Jeff was checking the line when a big snowstorm hit. Visibility had dropped to 100 yards or less. I was in my room at home doing homework and began to worry. I decided to go check the trap line and make sure he was okay. It took me about 20 minutes to get to the first trap. I could see that he had been there; then I checked the second trap. It was between traps three and four that I saw he had lost his way. He was headed onto the airport property; in the fast falling snow he had gotten confused. I kept moving faster 'cause I knew he was headed toward the runways. Then I saw by his tracks that he wasn't alone. He had been joined by a dog — a good-sized dog. They were walking together in the blizzard. I was getting closer, but I was still at least 10 minutes behind them. Visibility was down to 50 yards and no matter how confident you are, you begin to doubt yourself and your location in those conditions. I began to call for Jeff, and suddenly my calls were drowned out by the sound of a low flying, landing plane. Its engines roared not far above my head. Within minutes, I saw Jeff and a beautiful Irish setter walking directly toward me.

"Wow, what are you doing out here?" he asked.

"Lookin' for you. I saw what the storm was doing and figured you might need help."

"Boy, did I get lost. I got the first three traps checked and then I took a wrong turn. I don't know how I could have, but then this dog showed up and I kept going and he came along. Well, then that plane almost landed on me, and I knew I was going the wrong direction. So I turned around."

"We'll be okay," I said. "Who's the dog?"

"I don't know, but I think he's my guardian angel. I'm gonna make sure he gets a big bone tonight. I bet this dog could find pheasants."

I looked at the setter and saw a leather collar on his neck with some metal dangling below it. I was sure it was identification. By the time we finished out the trap line, it was dark. We now had a half-mile walk home. We had two muskrats and a fox — not too bad. The dog was very well behaved and even knew how to heel.

"Well," Jeff said, "he's half yours. You've always wanted a dog."

"Not this way, Jeff. He's not mine or yours."

We walked silently. We were about two blocks from home, by Bossen Field, the snow was getting deep, but the street lights were on. I could see quite well, and at that point I realized that the Irish setter no longer had a collar.

DIRK

Those situations – Duke and the dog Jeff stole —
were the closest I would ever get to having a dog
as a kid. Jeff and I drifted apart. Things just
weren't the same anymore. We sold our traps. My
sister and I pursued music, sports, travel, summer
camps, adventuring, student government, theater.
We enjoyed a good life with caring parents —
but without a dog. My mother always knew that
as we got older and left the house, the dog would
become her responsibility. Bonnie and I would
just have to wait till adulthood to fulfill our
childhood dream. In my mid-twenties opportunities began to surface.

Dogs perceive quickly where they are and are
not welcome. They can distinguish people who
like dogs from those who don't. They sense fear,

aggression, affection, people's moods and even their state of health. Years later, when my sister was married and working as a summer-stock actress at the Bemidji playhouse, there was a half-Lab stray that hung around the theater they named Dirk the Dog. Bonnie's husband, Gerry, was the theater director and the troupe included a steady stream of bright, young, talented performers, many of whom would make their living by acting, writing and directing. The whole crew fed Dirk, but the actress Michelle Barber looked after him the most. He was likeable, well mannered and he looked to me like he might have some hunting potential. By now I was in my twenties, my mother had sadly passed away, my dad lived alone and, as the theater season wrapped up, Dirk the Dog's fate became uncertain. Dad and I decided we'd make Dirk ours.

In those days, I was traveling a lot throughout the United States and so Dad and Dirk were spending a lot of time together. Upon my return from one trip, I dished up some food for Dirk, which he utterly ignored. I've never believed in forcing dogs to eat, so I just noticed the behavior and did nothing else. Later, I heard my dad on the telephone, and then he yelled to me, "Are you gonna be here tonight for dinner?" I yelled back "no" and he continued his phone conversation — he was ordering pizza.

"Okay, sorry, we'll need two medium pizzas, one with pepperoni, sausage, mushrooms and the other all-dressed. How long will that be? Okay, thanks," he said, hanging up.

As I came to join Dirk and Dad, the pizza-delivery guy arrived with their order. It was suddenly clear why Dirk had snubbed my dog food. He had become devoted to take-out and delivery. I watched in amazement as my dad took the pepperoni, sausage and mushroom pizza and placed it on the kitchen table. He then carefully opened the all-dressed pie and put it on the floor for the dog.

"Dad," I said. "Does he eat pizza all the time?"

Big Al turned to me and said, "Only on Fridays and Tuesdays." He grabbed a slice, took a big bite and said, "Actually, I think he prefers Mexican, but he's no slouch with General Tao and fried rice, either."

As much as I knew better, I didn't say a word. These two were really happy together, devoted pals who gave each other devotion, affection and a sense of purpose.

When Big Al had his heart attack that winter, Dirk stayed beside him as he curled up in fear and writhed in agony. As my cousin Gordy drove my dad to the hospital, Dirk lay right on the floor of the car next to him and then remained at the foot of Big Al's bed until he returned home. They went together like milk and cookies — and sometimes they'd share those, too!

In early September, I like to go grouse hunting, and Dirk loved to romp and chase birds in the field. Now, this mutt was a long way from the high-test, fine-bred, pedigreed dogs to which I would become committed; this was a half-breed, an untrained wanderer with an experienced palate but not a fine-tuned nose. When I went to pick up my girlfriend Kath to head off on our hunting trip, I had Dirk packed into the tiny backseat of my Fiat Spyder, which he completely filled. When we got to her apartment, she wasn't there yet, so Dirk and I let ourselves in. As I waited, an idea struck me. This would be a good time to give Dirk a bath. I found strawberry-scented shampoo, grabbed the dog and filled the tub, assuming he'd be happy because he had always loved water. I soon discovered that a dog doesn't necessarily associate a bathtub with pleasant memories and, before you could say "bad idea," he was out of the tub and running all over the apartment. He was dripping wet and as he neared Kath's couch, he decided to shake. He distributed water evenly onto the couch, the floor, the coffee table, the chair and two walls. The apartment began to take on a musty strawberry odor that would inspire most people to avoid the fruit for several years. I tried to grab him, but he evaded me and launched into her bedroom. Uncharacteristically, he jumped on the bed, which wouldn't have been quite so bad if he hadn't knocked over a potted plant along the way, so he left muddy paw prints everywhere he stepped.

As I approached the bed, he leapt to the floor on the other side and stood still. When I moved around the bed, he jumped over it and romped through the whole apartment. Just as I regained control, Kath came home. Her silence was deafening. There were suds, water, dirt and dog prints all over, the dog was wet and the bed was muddy, but the worst part was the synthetic strawberry smell permeating the whole apartment. With amazing good humor, we cleaned up Dirk, the bed and the bathroom and, an hour later, we were packed up and in the cramped Fiat Spyder to drive five hours north for grouse.

The next morning, I went out for a run with Dirk along beautiful Lake Superior. Grand Marais, Minnesota, may be one of my favorite places. I was a canoe guide in the area for three years and have always loved it there. After the run, I fed Dirk (dog food) and cleaned up. Then as I was packing to go hunting for the day, I realized Dirk was gone — vanished. I searched the small town for an hour and finally went to the sheriff's office. I reported Dirk the Dog was missing and went hunting, hoping they'd have him on my return, but no such luck. Saturday night was melancholy. When a dog disappears (and in the last 30 years it has happened to me numerous times), your feelings are a curious mix of sadness and anger. There is a part of you that's mad at the dog or whoever you think is responsible for the situation and a part of you experiences the sadness of their absence. I was sure he'd show up.

Sunday morning came, however, without a sign. I went hunting, checked back in the afternoon, but the sheriff didn't have Dirk. It was time to go and I was traveling to New York the next day. I left contact information with the sheriff and reluctantly left town.

Three days later Big Al got the call. I was still in New York. He reached me and told me to call the sheriff in Grand Marais. I called, full of anxiety, fear and regret. "This is Bill Urseth," I said, welling up, "I was told to call."

"Yes," the sheriff said. "There was a group of 'dognappers' working our county. Of course, we didn't know it until you left. They were stealing hunting dogs, nine altogether. When we caught 'em, they only had eight dogs and yours was the one missing. So we asked the crooks if they had another dog at some point, and they said that yes, they did, a black Lab-like dog that attacked them as they put another dog in the kennel, and he got away. One of them said the dog kinda smelled like strawberries.

"We asked them where this happened and they told us so we drove out there and sure enough, we found your dog. He came right to us."

"Wow, that's great," I said. "We'll come pick him up. Thanks."

"Just one second," the sheriff said.

"Yeah, sure," I replied.

"My wife wants to know how you get a dog to smell that way. She'd like our Pekinese to smell like that."

I told him that I'd drop off a bottle of the shampoo when we picked up Dirk the Dog, which we did, but we've never had a bottle of strawberry shampoo of our own since.

WHAT BREED?

Due largely to the fact that I just loved dogs, I had no breed bias when it came time for me to get serious about getting one. I had been exposed to terriers, wirehairs, golden retrievers, Labs, Weimaraners, spaniels, setters, Chesapeakes, boxers, bulldogs, shepherds, even Chihuahuas, and I liked them all. Now that I was maturing and becoming more and more practical, though, it made sense to make a basic decision. Do I love dogs, or do I love what dogs can do? I realized that I tended to the latter category; as I understood more about what a working dog could be, I was drawn to the purposefulness they represented.

Shepherding dogs fascinated me. The smartest of all breeds, shepherds of all delineations have lived close to man in a very symbiotic way for at least 50,000 years. They can protect, alert, fight, guide and herd livestock, poultry or even people. They work alone or in teams and possess an intelligence that can exceed those of most other dogs and even some people. There's one German shepherd that can identify over 200 words, retrieving objects to prove it, which is about as many words as a two-year-old child. As I saw shepherds working ducks on a football field and herding them from one goal post to the next in competition, I was intrigued by the training process, the discipline, the team work — by the entire process. As I saw how they coordinated efforts to move a herd of sheep through an obstacle course, I was as enthralled as most would be at a soccer match.

There are so many ways that canines and people combine to achieve outcomes. On my first coon hunt, I realized how instinctive these breeds were. The blue ticks, red bones and black-and-tans would perceive the coon scent and then in evening's darkness work their trails, for hours if necessary, through whatever terrain lay ahead, all with the intent and purpose to tree that coon and bring it to corner. The hunts were so much fun I'd lose track of time and soon it would be 3:00 a.m. or the sun would be rising in the east. The tough, athletic, highly instinctive coonhound would seem to never tire or vary from purpose. They were easy to admire.

When terriers are brought out of the house and treated like field dogs, the results are amazing. Smart, tenacious, clever and quick, their noses are keen and they have amazing verve. I've seen Jack Russells track a wounded boar six hours after a rainstorm over the most unforgiving Texas countryside, baying them up cleverly so as to keep themselves safe. I've seen them in Africa take on dangerous game, again using their phenomenal nose and keen smarts to track, locate and hold bucks, cats, even Cape buffalo. The tunneling terriers seem to have no fear of the tight, dark places where rats may thrive and don't shirk the most dangerous feats when given the chance.

The speed of chase dogs produces sheer excitement and it's thrilling to think of their role on the hunt in earlier days — chasing stags or deer or predators throughout Europe and Asia. Greyhounds, whippets, elk hounds and wolf hounds all raced in pursuit of quarry.

Or the tracking hounds whose noses exceeded even the most refined bird dog or terrier. They were able to work old scents or new scents and differentiate between the two when necessary. The role of the hounds by any name — blood, basset or Spanish — was a valuable part of the hunt and would frequently put the chase dogs back into the game. Chase hounds, like beagles and fox hounds, would be at the core of a hunt's excitement and would ultimately act as the hammer of conclusion.

Humans began to divide bird-hunting dogs by increasingly specialized functions such as finding, flushing and retrieving. By 1870, the pointers and setters were well defined, as were the flushers and retrievers. At this time, dog breeding was a function of the aristocracy, and they maintained handlers to tend to their breeding programs and manage their kennels. Because game was owned by the landholders in Europe, hunting was limited to aristocrats and their guests or the occasional gamekeeper or poacher. When the Franco-Prussian war ended in 1870, the new settlements made French hunting land available to upper-middle-class Germans. While affluent enough to be able to buy guns, travel and enjoy leisure time, this new class of hunter couldn't afford highly specialized, large kennels of pointers, setters, flushers and retrievers. They wanted one or two dogs that could do it all: find and retrieve game. This created a demand for new, less-specialized breeds for the upland hunter and water fowler. For the first time since the dark ages, humans were seeking a versatile dog that could accomplish what had previously taken a dozen dogs to do. As shotgun technology improved, and as birds and small game on legal land became more accessible, the sport flourished and the need for the all-around dog grew. Among the resulting breeds were the German shorthair pointer, Brittany, English pointer, Irish setter, English setter, Weimaraner, German wirehair and Vizsla on the pointing side. On the flushing side were the golden retriever, Labrador, Chesapeake, Springer spaniel, cocker spaniel and flat-coat retriever.

In the beginning, these breeds were largely created through a "mongrelization" process that combined certain traits and breeds of established hound and water-dog breeds to produce the new breeds being sought. This is how the German shorthair and wirehair *(drahthaar)* were introduced. By blending the Spanish hound with the foxhound, the speedy greyhound and the English pointer, the German shorthair emerged. These dogs were versatile, athletic, biddable and soon became very popular. Their popularity was built on the simple fact that most of them could do what they were advertised to do — find and retrieve game, track blood, catch and retrieve fur and swim with excellent endurance. To a great extent, these are the same standards by which many versatile dogs are judged to this day and as a result, what most breeders strive to achieve.

Before I ever bought my first dog, I studied, saw and admired many breeds in order to decide where I, then a guy in my late twenties, was finally headed. In the process, I vacillated between the golden retriever (which I still think is the prettiest breed I've ever seen), the German wirehair (which is one of the ugliest breeds I've ever seen) and the German shorthair (which is never as pretty as the golden, but never as ugly as the wirehair). The decisive factors were the athleticism of the shorthair, the general lack of dysplasia in the breed, the much larger gene pool compared to wirehairs and, finally, there was Jenny.

Now that I had decided that my dog was going to do something, I knew I'd rather have it chase birds than dummies, varmints or coons at night, or herd ducks, or track blood trails, or drag trails or convicts. What I wanted was a living, breathing, bird-finding machine that would be loyal, loving, welcoming and generally uplifting. Tom Choate, a lifelong hunting partner of mine, owned a shorthair named Jenny at this time. We went hunting in northeast Iowa and I had the chance to see what a GSP (German shorthair pointer) could do. We hunted ground I knew because I had hunted it alone many times and I knew how many birds to expect. With Jenny, all bets were off. She found birds, pointed birds, held birds, retrieved birds, tracked cripples, dug them out of thick cover, snowbanks and, in a feat that went over the top for me, she held point for over five minutes on a few blades of grass covered with snow. Tom and I kicked around and kicked around. It was obvious to us there was nothing there, but sure enough, when we finally walked away, out flew a hen pheasant from beneath the snow. My love affair with shorthairs had begun.

MERRY MAKER

The first dog we got (because at this point Kath and I were very close), was a Wisconsin GSP named Merry Maker. She was four years old, fully trained and living in a well-recommended kennel. We drove to pick her up in my Fiat Spyder convertible — with no kennel and no pickup truck, I looked more like a preppie than a sportsman. I'll never forget how Merry Maker's ears flopped in the wind as we drove back from Wisconsin. She sat up in that small back seat looking all around like a beauty queen in a parade. Every once in a while, she would lean forward and give us kisses just to remind us she was our dog now. She had never been anybody's dog before; she had always lived in a kennel and hunted for money in front of paying guests on a preserve. When the day was done, most other dogs would go home to their dog beds and families, get pats and kisses, dinner and treats, but Merry would just get dog food alone in her cinderblock kennel. Starting that day, all that changed.

She hunted hard and very successfully; the more we'd hunt, the better we'd get at it, and the more time I'd allocate to our quality time together. Sometimes she'd range too far, but what I found was that if I stayed with her, we'd get more birds than we would if I hacked her back to where I was or where I thought there were birds. So, slowly, she was changing me and I was learning to hunt the dog, not take the dog hunting. After all, she was the one who was bred to find pheasants, not me. Hell, I was an ad man, a promotion guy, not a dog, so I let her do her job. It amazes me how many hunters think they know better and over-handle their dogs.

To extend my hunting season beyond the native-bird season and give Merry more field work, I joined a hunt club and that let us hunt all winter and into the spring. We'd go out at minus 15 and minus 20 degrees Fahrenheit because we loved to do it. When dogs are miserable from the cold, they will tell you, believe me. Being a cold-winter guy all my life, I've had plenty of dogs communicate to me, "Hey, boss, this is really cold, so no hunting today." Most often I respect their wishes or at least cut the workout short.

How do dogs communicate? Dogs speak surprisingly well with their eyes and through their actions.

If you open the kennel door in your truck and the dog doesn't come barreling out, but instead lies or waits or generally hesitates, he or she is telling you something. If, when they hit the ground, they start limping or biting at their paws instead of running normally, they're communicating.

Remember, dogs are hard-wired to not show pain. They are pack animals and any injury announces weakness in a pack, which can lead to change of order. The hesitations, limps or paw biting are all indications of a weakness that your dog is trying to hide from the alpha male or female in their pack, which is you, the boss. So watch for it. When Merry had enough, which was rare, she would lie down and put her front paws over her eyes. She seemed to think that if she couldn't see me, I couldn't see her.

The greatest thing about falling in love is the development of this non-verbal communication. It's the most important interaction that we frequently share with loved ones, much more important, intimate and expressive than the spoken word, which is greatly overrated. Dogs make all their most significant expressions of affection in this way. Only in hokey television shows, corny movies or Disney cartoons do dogs express the affirmative with barks. Dogs convey contentment, gratitude and attachment silently. When they do bark, it's to say, "let me out," "I'm hungry," "I'm caught, boss." As with all generalizations, there are a few exceptions, but very few.

Merry was a lover-girl and she would sneak attention and affection whenever possible. If I was standing, she'd sidle right up next to me so it was easy for me to scratch her ears. If I was taking a nap, she'd lie as close as possible, with her face by my face. If I was driving, she'd kiss me every few minutes.

Merry was supposed to be the beginning of The Line. We had every intention now of having multiple dogs and breeding German shorthair pointers, so after a couple of years we decided to breed her. We carefully studied pedigrees, listened to opinions, got ideas, theories, gossip, studied offspring and hunted with potential sires. Finally, out of dozens of suitors,

Merry was to mate with a handsome, accomplished male a little her junior who was owned by a prominent veterinarian. When the two were introduced for their courtship, Merry Maker, the loveable kisser, lunged at his throat like Mike Tyson in a bad mood. I had never seen, heard or experienced anything like it. Caught completely by surprise, the vet and the breeding hands on site tore them apart, but not without blood.

"Wow, what do you make of that?" I asked.

"Oh, no big deal," the experts all agreed. "Just a little early, I guess."

They put them together the next day, but I wasn't there. I was told that "she really tore him up this time." Since I saw her really tear him up the first time, I couldn't imagine this second round. The event was, once again, minimized, and a third attempt was planned. Later I learned that the breeders were intending to essentially facilitate a rape without my knowledge or that of the vet. Fully restrained with her neck in a noose, she put on such a vicious show that the stud couldn't get himself aroused and the effort failed. Today, breeders would automatically turn to artificial insemination in this situation, but not so at that time. A.I. wasn't common then, so Merry was never bred. "The Line" was to be ruled by the Virgin Queen until her death, because though she was always the alpha leader of the pack, she was never its genetic progenitor.

By Merry's ninth birthday I knew I'd need a new dog soon. I was told that Merry would hunt to the age of 11 or so. With hindsight, this was an optimistic estimate; while she hunted till 12, I've since found that dogs are pretty well finished by 10 or so. I began my search.

At about the same time, I was approached to buy the hunt club where I was a member, an idea I found very appealing. When I told Kath that the owner had asked me to buy it, she said, "I hope you told him no," and changed the subject. Now, 25 years later, there are times when I wish I'd followed her advice, but for the most part, I know I made the right decision. Owning this club gave me a chance to professionally see, watch, learn and work with dogs as few people ever can.

Just before I bought the club, it held the first Minnesota State Pheasant Hunting Championship. It was run with a simple set of rules that created an innovative new game that became Tournament Hunting. Two men, one dog, 20 acres of field containing six birds. The idea was to get the six birds in the shortest amount of time with the fewest shots. Today there are more complicated rules and various leagues and conferences, but in 1984 the game was very straightforward.

Over 30 teams showed up for this first state championship, and pointers and flushers ran against each other. There would be only one winner. The habit of letting the dog hunt would pay off that Saturday in December as nine-year-old Merry Maker ran with the reckless abandon she was famous for and found six pheasants in 12 minutes, which my partner Gil Roscoe and I shot for Merry and she retrieved for us. She was first Minnesota State Champion — the Virgin Queen began the tradition of winning for a Line that still did not exist.

JÄGER

Jäger was only six weeks old when we first saw her. She was the offspring of a professional hunting dog and the stud that Merry Maker had terrorized. Jäger was the runt of the litter, but she was the most active, the quickest, slept the least, ate the most and always found the best teat. She moved the bigger dogs out to get her own way, despite her size. She followed a bird wing on a fishing rod more keenly than the rest and cuddled despite her typical puppy A.D.D. The litter's owner had made it clear that he wanted these pups sold before the deal to buy the club went through, so I wasn't going to get Jäger by default or as chattel. She needed to be a cash purchase, one we were glad to do. I swear that the energy some dogs give off brings a smile on a bad day, keeps you moving when you're dead tired, lifts your hopes when you're recovering from illness or injury and makes the most ordinary day seem like you've won the lottery.

Introducing new dogs — including puppies — to the pack is a process and an art. We were the only pack Merry had ever known so she loved us and we were a happy three-some. Nobody had consulted her about a new addition, especially one with the energy of Jäger. The hair on her back went up the minute we snuck that eight-week-old sack of fur into the house.

This was a big old Victorian house built in 1878. There was plenty of space, but we all slept in the same bedroom. Every morning, Merry and I would run an hour or more through the city parks. It was our special time together, not as good as hunting, but pretty close. Suddenly here was this twerp — small, precocious and intrusive. Merry seemed to be wondering, "How could Bill and Kath do this to me?" Jäger quickly developed the habit of "Pearl Harboring" Merry, which is not a very politically correct description, but a very accurate one. She would sneak up on the sleeping or resting Merry and run full-blast right at her, jumping on her or banging into her head. After such an attack, Merry would, depending on her mood, get up and wrassle, grab the little rat by the scruff and shake her or growl ferociously in order to re-establish her alpha role. Then she would go back to sleep. The growls were terrifying and all the scarier knowing what Merry had done to Jäger's father. Merry kept order, maintained the pack and never really hurt Jäger, who she grew to like.

You can tell if dogs like each other, don't like each other or are ambivalent. Dogs that like each other cuddle, play, sleep nose to butt with each other, share dog beds, kennels, and choose to be together. Dogs that don't get along fight, taunt, avoid each other, growl and rarely (or never) cuddle, play, share or sleep together. Dogs that are ambivalent use the pack order to insulate themselves and growl without intent to harm as a way to keep distance. Merry liked Jäger and Jäger liked Merry.

Most people don't realize it, but having two dogs isn't much more difficult than having one. Going from no dog to one dog is a big jump; from one dog to two dogs is a very small change. They tend to take care of each other. Moving from two animals to three is a big change again and from there having four, five, six or seven are small incremental changes. The pack maintains its own order and related sanity.

At four months, and way ahead of schedule, Jäger got her first training lesson. She had basic obedience down like "here," "fetch," and "whoa," but nothing more advanced. Kath, Terry Correll (the club manager), his wife Karen and I went out with six chukkar partridges to train Jäger. We released the birds into a hunting field and let Jäger out. She ran to the first bird, pointed it, we shot it, she retrieved it right to hand. Then she found the second bird; we shot that one too and she retrieved it. The same followed with birds three, four and five. Jäger then found bird six. She held a very stylish point for a four-month-old runt. We flushed the bird and shot it; she ran over and retrieved it to hand. This was the first time she'd ever hunted. She had just gone through bird and gun intro, pointed birds, been steadied, retrieved and retrieved to hand in 20 minutes. At this point Terry said to me, "Do you want this dog to sit?"

I said, "No, I don't like my pointers to sit."

"Well, then, I don't know what else we could teach this

dog," he said, as if we had taught the dog anything in the first place. To this day we brag about being the guys that trained Jäger, knowing full well we didn't do a damn thing — and then we smile.

At six months, we took Jäger to the Iowa-Illinois Championship down near Cedar Rapids, Iowa. Gil Roscoe and I were competing Merry and his dog Tank seriously, but brought Jäger for laughs and 'cause she was just fun to have around. Merry and Tank were both good, *real* good, and we were getting a reputation since we'd won the Minnesota State Pheasant Championship. The tournament paid to third place, and on Sunday morning Merry and Tank were in second and third place. So we entered Jäger, all six months and 40 pounds of her. As we took her to the line, we could see people laughing, joking, smirking.

"Wow, I'd like to follow that little pipsqueak in the field," I heard one guy say, implying that she'd be leaving all the birds behind for the next team, thus creating an advantage.

Well, the pipsqueak charged into that field and had her first two birds in three minutes. As she retrieved the second bird, the judge said with a heavy drawl, "How old is that dog anyway?"

I said, "Six months."

In minutes she struck another point and then another and another. As she retrieved bird number five, and with only one bird left, the judge looked at me.

"Wouldn't want to sell that dog, would you?" he drawled.

I didn't respond as I raced behind Jäger to bird six. When it was all over she took second and knocked Tank into fourth. We took half the prize money for second and third. No one laughed, smirked or joked as we came in. The judge wasn't the only one who wanted to buy that dog. The untrained, six-month-old pipsqueak had bounced over 80 top-notch pointers and flushers out of the money that day and The Line truly began. There was now a genetic seed. Merry had been the spiritual start, but Jäger was the biddable huntress who would be the core of The Line.

JÄGER'S MISSING

From my stint in the Marine Corps onwards, I was always committed to morning exercise. For much of my life, I ran every morning. I would typically head out around 6:30 a.m., and though the distances have varied, I'm usually out for an hour or two. There have been years when I was training for distance races and marathons where the runs would be even longer. From the time the dogs showed up in my life, one, two or even three would come with me for my morning jaunt. This is our special time together, and they love the exercise as much as I do. I rigged up a special contraption from a weightlifting belt that went around my waist — I attached the dog leashes to it, so the pull of the dogs would be more at my center of gravity. While this rig sounds treacherous, it really worked slickly, and even on icy ground or in snow, I never got tangled or fell because of it. The dogs looked forward to these morning runs almost as much as they did a day in the field.

As we went, they'd hold their heads high and move at a gait that matched mine. It was a trot-type speed and they would posture their bodies like the proudest racer on the track at Saratoga. Somehow they knew how good-looking they were, how they caught the eye of all the people we passed, those in the cars driving by and other dogs who were usually alone, not part of a team.

I figured out that in my running career I ran over 56,000 miles, about one-and-a-half times around the earth. Most of the running was done with Merry, Jäger, Cent, Gretchen, Gus, Liesel, Fritz, Mixx, Abby, Bernie, Hank, Haley or Scent along, depending on the era and the generation that I was lucky enough to be sharing my time with.

There was one part of my run on the north side of Cedar Lake (right in the heart of the city) near some seldom-used railroad tracks where I would let Jäger off the leash and let her run. In those days there were no leash laws. One morning, just as I was about to hook her back up and head back on to the running path, Jäger was attacked by a big dog. She was always small and quick and she usually got away, but as she ran like the dickens, she was moving away from me as well. I searched for her for an hour. To go home and tell Kath she was lost was as hard as anything I'd ever do. We were both weak in the knees and uncertain of what to do next. Suddenly, all the tricks of my youth for finding and re-placing dogs came back to me. I played back the situation, circumstances, the place where it happened, where I'd looked already, everything. We quickly made and printed signs and called the authorities; we began to put up the signs, knock on doors and pray. We checked our porch and the doors to our house every hour to see if she had found her way back to us — with no luck. She was gone for 36 hours.

Almost two days later, the phone rang and Kath answered. An elderly lady began to ask questions. She eventually said that the dog was dazed when she found her on her back porch and that she brought her in and fed her, and now the dog seemed to be very happy there. With terror in her heart, Kath realized this person had fallen for little Jäger and might be calling only to take the mystery away, not to return her.

Assertively she said "Where are you? I'd love to come see my dog." There was no answer. "Please, where are you? I miss that dog so much. I need to see her." There was another pause, then the woman said, "You're right, it's your dog. I'm only wishing that she was mine."

Jäger had probably been hit by a car after she ran, which explains why she didn't come to my calls and why I couldn't find her. She then crawled to the house of this woman who was a Good Samaritan, even if a reluctant one. She probably regretted her phone call after she made it.

TRAINERS

The Minnesota Horse and Hunt Club — which I had purchased with my longtime friend and business partner, Corky Hall — has been expanding since we bought it. It had grown to include over 700 acres of woods, fields, sloughs, potholes and hunt cover. We had built overnight lodging; three separate dog kennels that could hold over 90 dogs; a 35-stall horse barn; and the second sporting clays course in the country. Sporting clays is a shooting game where you move through a course, kind of like golf with a shotgun. The bar and restaurant served wild game and other country fare that hunters and their guests could enjoy. It was only 45 minutes from downtown Minneapolis and downtown St. Paul and only 25 minutes from the airport. We wanted it to be a special place for the outdoorsmen and their families, and that's what we worked toward every day.

Now that we had purchased the Hunt club, we began to emphasize dogs, breeding and training.

The first dog trainer we had at the club was a fellow that I found and recruited from Ohio. His name was Dick. He and his family moved from Ohio to the club and lived right on the grounds. At the time I was naïve to the fact that a lot of dog trainers become trainers because they get along better with dogs than they do with people. Dick had been with us for about six months when I got a call at my office from a very angry customer.

"Are you Bill Urseth?" the voice demanded.

"Yes," I said.

"Well, I want you to know that dog trainer of yours is an evil, cruel man and that he told me he's going to shoot my dog!" The male voice still had no name, but it certainly had a temper.

"He said what?" I asked.

"He said he's going to shoot my dog, the one I have in for training."

"Okay, let me get your name and number. I'll get to the bottom of this and call you back."

I went to see Dick in person since I didn't know him all that well yet and he was still somewhat new to the operation.

"Dick, I've got a situation that we need to talk about," is how I started out.

"Sure, Bill, what's up?"

"I got a phone call from a fellow today. A Mr. Thomas, who I gather has a dog in for training."

"Yeah, that's right."

"Well, the guy said that you told him you were going to shoot his dog."

Dick smiled and said, "Oh hell, Bill, I wouldn't waste one of my bullets on that dawg. I never said that."

"What did you say?" I asked.

"He brought the dog in for ten weeks of training and now it's week number four. He comes out to see how the dog's coming along and says that it doesn't seem like the dog has improved much. He's insulting me, acting like I can't train dogs. So I said I can only get out what's already in. You know what I mean. If a dog hasn't got it, I can't make him into something he ain't. Why, Bill, I had to train it to point!" With that, Dick stuck one hand out in front of him and one hand out behind him, impersonating a pointing dog.

"Bill, if a dog can't point by instinct, it shouldn't be a pointing dog! Then this guy says to me, 'If it were your dog, Dick, what would you do with it?'

"So, I told him. 'If it were my dog, I'd shoot it.' And I would. I'd be damned if I'd put my money into training something that stupid."

At this point I was quite certain that he hadn't threatened to shoot the man's dog. I was also quite certain that the dog probably was a slow learner and very certain that Dick had shot something alright and that was his own foot. He totally lacked bedside manner and that's either a crippling wound or a fatal flaw for a dog trainer. Dick and I separated ways within a week.

We then went through two more dog trainers, one of whom loved talking about "Jack" everywhere he went. He'd say, "Jack and I will be there in a minute" or "Jack and I will come over tonight and we'll talk dogs." "Me and Jack are assessing the Lab. We'll be through shortly." The core of the problem was that "Jack" was, in fact, Jack Daniels himself, and was constantly in the man's pocket, on his breath and in his bloodstream. So I fired both him and Jack.

There was another trainer who had mixed feeling about purebreds. "I sometimes think the best dogs of all are mutts and crossbreds," he'd say. Not discreetly, but to customers who had fine, purebred pups. His own collection of mutts were miscellaneous Airedale-Lab crosses, setters crossed with beagles and a pit bull–golden retriever cross, which had to be the most conflicted dog in history, one that would lovingly lick the bite marks it had inflicted. This loser was hired while I was on an extended road trip, and his future grew dim once I saw the menagerie he had collected and when he unwisely offered to explain his mutt theory after a six-pack of malt liquor.

Finding really good dog trainers is tough to do. When I first met Terry Holzinger, I liked him right away. Terry had worked with one of the country's great dog trainers, Tom Dokken, who trains about 30 miles away. Terry Holzinger worked only with hunting dogs, either pointers or flushers, and no other types at all. This specialization is important with trainers; it not only builds expertise, but it reduces training times and diagnostic issues. At the time, Terry was young but focused, and the meeting would be fortuitous. He wanted to lease the kennel, not have a job. He wanted to build a business and he knew how to deal with people and how to deal with dogs. That is the magic combination that so few trainers have. He came to the club in 1987 and has never left — he is a great trainer and assessor of dog talent.

CENT VON ESTERFELD

I knew that if The Line was going to move forward the way that I dreamed it would, I needed an eye-turning, pulse-quickening, bird-finding assemblage of pure brawn. My businesses in those days were doing very well, and I had established some interests in West Germany, as well. I audaciously commissioned the head of the West German, German Shorthair Society to determine the world's greatest German shorthair under four years old. In true Germanic fashion he took this project very seriously. He studied data, trials and pedigrees to achieve an accurate outcome and to maximize his fees. Ultimately, he ascertained through his methodology of quantitative and qualitative analysis and observation that the two-year-old Cent Von Esterfeld was the "best

German shorthair in the world." Cent was living at the time with Herr Schulman in the Frankfurt area of West Germany. He was 82 pounds of solid muscle and as athletic as Bruce Jenner. In fact, he too was a bit of a decathlete, because the German K.S. (Klemansieger) Trials require a dog to find birds, retrieve birds, track blood, track fur and retrieve a nine-pound fox to hand over a land-and-water obstacle course. This is what Schulman had trained Cent to do, and he excelled at it. Cent thrived on the difficulty and used his perfect conformation to make the endurance contest look easy. This remarkable dog had caught the attention of the world's most discerning judges.

Armed with the information from the society's head, I moved forward with my approach to Herr Schulman. Speaking fair German, I approached Cent's unsuspecting owner out of nowhere with a simple proposal. Introducing myself, I said, "My name is Bill Urseth and I live in the United States. I love dogs, but most of all I love what dogs can do. I've heard of your dog Cent Von Esterfeld, and I understand he's very good. I'd like to buy him from you. If you sold him to me, I promise you I'd keep him his whole life, treat him well and campaign him to make him the best that he can be."

I rambled further. "I'm 35 years old and want to develop a great line of German shorthairs in the United States. He would be the base of my program."

"Thank you for calling," he began. "It's very flattering that you would call, and Cent is very special. I'm gathering I could name my price —"

"That's right," I interrupted.

"But it's not money that I want. It's a great dog and I have one now, so I would never sell."

The words hit me like a ton of bricks. A *no!* I couldn't

believe it, but then I realized that I should have expected a *no* and not a *yes*. Germans are unlike the British, who tend to maintain a distance between themselves and their dogs. Rarely do the British allow hunting breeds into the house. They keep the dogs outside and view them as utilitarian creatures, not family. In the U.S., we tend to buy a dog and when they pass we bury them as members of the family. The Germans go even further. The dogs are not only welcome in the house, but they also bring them along to the restaurant where they lie peacefully under the table while their masters drink bier at the Bierstube or dine at the restaurant. They walk in the evenings as people stroll through the streets. Cent had never eaten commercial dog food, eating only fresh meat in a country where meat is very expensive. How vain of me, how self-centered that I would expect a *yes* when *no* was the more sensible answer.

"If you should ever change your mind and decide you'd like to sell him, please call me. Here's my number." I began to wind down the call. An hour later I called the head of the society and said, "Well, who do you think is number two?" He went back to work on my search.

Two months went by and I was back in the United States when the phone rang. "Herr Urseth?" the weak voice on the other end of the phone inquired.

"Yes," I said.

"This is Herr Schulman."

"Hello. How are you?"

"Not so good, I'm afraid. I've had a heart attack and I now know that Cent would be better off with you than with me. You promised me you would campaign him and make him good, didn't you, Herr Urseth?"

"Yes, I did. I promised that, and he will be the base of my Line," I added.

"Then he is yours because I can no longer do that. He would just be the dog of an old man if he stays with me. He's so much more than that."

We agreed on a price of $5,000, which — while it was expensive — was less than one might think, because at the time the Deutschmark was 66 cents to the U.S. dollar. Years later this transaction wouldn't have been possible for me.

Within weeks, Cent Von Esterfeld, the number one ranked German shorthair pointer in the world, was on his way to the United States of America. The Line now had its Virgin Queen (Merry), Jäger (the cute as a button prodigy) and Cent Von Esterfeld. I was feeling very, very good. Cent would fly from Frankfurt to Boston, then on to Minneapolis. His flight to Minneapolis was delayed so he was cooped up in a "kennelaire" for twenty hours. He was so proud that he neither peed nor defecated in his crate. It would have been beneath him. When he finally arrived and emerged from his confinement outside the airport, he was relieved in a variety of ways.

When I first saw him, he exceeded the promise of his photographs and my imagination. Only in person do you catch the muscle tone, the broad chest and narrow behind; the long legs become more obvious, the size of the feet more clear. When you touched him, you felt the softness of his large ears, the thick oiliness of his coat and you experienced the admiring glance he cast as you patted his head. We snuck Cent into the house because of the hour, and we did not want to introduce Merry and Jäger until the right time; knowing Merry's history with males, this was quite important.

That night, with his stomach full and after lots of petting time, Cent was in his kennelaire in the living room. He was the most beautiful, complete dog I'd ever seen since Duke. The other two were up in the second floor bedroom. In the middle of the night, Jäger had "to go" and she rushed down the stairs to get outside. She landed right in front of Cent's kennel and he woke up. At that moment he saw her for the first time. He came fully alert and, as if on point, he froze his body, then howled a sound I'd never heard before, nor have I since. It was high-pitched, variegated, like a wolf whistle. The tone revealed affection — raw genuine affection. At that moment, he fell in love with the cute little female we called Jäger. From that day forward, they would be pack mates, pals, parents, lovers, teammates, cuddlers, allies and even competitors, running against each other in tournaments. If either encountered danger or a fight broke out, they'd both be in it in a flash, never thinking of themselves, only of the other's safety. From that moment on they slept together, with Jäger's head using Cent's butt for a pillow or Cent curled up to keep Jäger warm. His howl was the most expressive sound I've ever heard a dog make. He was saying, "Wow, she's the cutest little thing I've ever seen and I'm glad to be in the USA!"

The introduction to Merry went pretty well, too, and Cent accepted his role in the pack obligingly. He was "number one in the world," but number three in this pack. These two girls ran the show, but he good-naturedly went along with them, never needing to assert his strength, size or power due to his total confidence and, in Jäger's case, unbridled affection.

ROY ROGERS VISITS
THE CLUB

When Cent arrived, he truly reached celebrity status as the outdoors and news media learned of his existence. There were newspaper articles, magazine stories and television features all about the world traveling shorthair that still had to be commanded in German because he "couldn't speak English." His commands were often similar, but not the same. *Sitzen* was sit, *abhor* was fetch, *essen* was eat, *komm* meant come, *suchen* was hunt 'em up. I actually continued to command him in German his entire life, which worked pretty well, because when I was running multiple dogs I could give him different commands than the others, if I wanted. He was so good-looking, people would stop on the street to comment, and ad agencies began to use him as a model for photo shoots. He took it all in stride and was of course oblivious to his fame, as long as his food bowl was full and Jäger was around for cuddling.

When I was a kid growing up in South Minneapolis hoping against all hope to have a dog someday, I would have never hoped so high as a dog like Cent. We were brought up as the first television generation. I can still remember life without TV and the day our first set arrived. It was a big wooden frame and a small black-and-white screen, more a piece of furniture than a television by today's standards. That TV brought images, hopes, dreams, stories, heroes and villains into our minds and because of it, we could think bigger and visualize a larger world. One of my top TV heroes was Roy Rogers. He was on Saturday morning and I never missed his show. He was quite a role model; in his world there was good and bad, heroes and villains, right and wrong. Roy was always good, always a hero and always right. He had a fine woman named Dale Evans, a sidekick named Gabby Hayes, a horse called Trigger, a Jeep named Nellybelle and, of course, a dog named Bullet. This ensemble would get up to all kinds of adventures every week and teach us simple values in the process. Why, Roy could even sing and each show ended with him singing his theme song "Happy Trails to You" (which I could sing by memory at any time).

In real life Roy and Dale lived on a ranch and raised a huge family of children they had adopted from all over the world. Roy loved horses, dogs and hunting. He seemed to live a life that exemplified family values and decency, much like the one he represented on TV.

Rob Evans was an active member of our club. He loved to entertain and was an able organizer who could bring people together. He became one of the country's top bow hunters and over the years helped raise millions of dollars for children's cancer research. He grew up in a very parallel way to me. He loved the outdoors, loved to hunt, valued dogs, had gone into the military and he also loved Roy Rogers. Rob heard that Roy was turning 75 years old, and he decided to invite Roy to the club to celebrate his birthday with a big hunt and party. He asked my opinion.

I said, "That would be great! Do you know him?"

"Nope, not personally, but I do know him very well, because he taught me so much as a kid."

Rob was right. Roy Rogers had taught us all a lot. Rob contacted Roy and the response was, "As long as I can bring my son Dusty along, too, I'll be there." The deal was set. Roy flew to Minnesota for his 75th birthday party and Rob planned a splendid event.

When the assignments were laid out, Rob decided that I should guide Roy Rogers on his pheasant hunts, which I was thrilled to do. Of course, this meant that Cent and Jäger would lead the way for the Singing Cowboy as he walked the hills and fields of the club. Roy and Dusty were staying in The Hunter's Lodge, a large log building with a big stone fireplace, high ceilings, a bar and huge table. While the meal would be up in the restaurant, aptly named Triggers, the appetizers would be served in The Hunter's Lodge.

Not unexpectedly, Roy took a liking to Cent immediately, and the big strong dog found bird after bird for Roy and the group, and retrieved them all flawlessly. When the first hunt was over, we went back to The Hunter's Lodge where venison hearts were soaking in one sink, moose liver in another and the staff had put various cheeses on the coffee tables as snacks.

As I approached the door Roy said, "Bill, why don't you bring Cent in? He's such a good boy."

"Okay, I will," was my quick response. With a saunter Cent entered the lodge, the only dog to be invited. He moved through the dozen or so guests, receiving the obligatory head pat and good dog comments. He was a perfect gentleman. Then Roy grabbed his guitar and sang "Happy Trails," the song that all of us boomers had grown up on. It was the song I had listened to every Saturday morning from the time I was six until I turned 12, and here was the guy who sang it, right there in front of me. At this stage of our lives many had become jaded, salty, even cynical, but at this moment on this beautiful fall day in 1987, in this log cabin after a good hunt, we were thrown back to our youth and all the idealism that it offered. We listened in awe as Roy Rogers sang "Happy Trails" to us.

As we focused our eyes on Roy, our minds drifted off to our childhoods and the memories of our youth. Evidently Roy wasn't ever as popular in Germany as he was with us Americans. With Roy as his diversion, Cent Von Esterfeld sidled over to the sink and hidden from view by the bar, jumped up on his hind legs and started first with the deer hearts. There were four of them. He then moved to the next sink where the moose livers were. There were two of them. Feeling a need to cleanse his palate, he meandered into the main room where he completely devoured the Stilton, Colby, Swiss, Boursin and Jarlsberg. Within two choruses of "Happy Trails," Cent had eaten 10 pounds of raw meat and two or three pounds of cheese.

I saw him grab the last piece of cheese and quickly moved toward him. I noticed the other plates were empty. I grabbed the plates and brought them to the sink. As Roy sang "keep smiling until then," I saw that the meat was also missing. At that point, Cent was right next to me and he burped. I double-checked the fridge to see if someone had moved the hearts and livers. They hadn't. It was quite clear that Cent had eaten everything.

When Roy finished singing, we all applauded. Some had tears in their eyes, which they tried to hide. Roy then walked outside onto the porch and we all followed, laughing, telling stories and reminiscing right up until lunch. Everyone then moved up to the restaurant and never noticed what the dog had done.

MAKING A DOG'S ACQUAINTANCE

After six months or so I was really beginning to know Cent, both his strengths and weaknesses. There are times when high-test hunting dogs bring their owners deep swellings of pride that can only be compared to having your kid voted valedictorian or your horse win a stakes race. Cent Von Esterfeld was the 82-pound, square-headed, sleekly built German Shorthair Pointer who could stir such emotions in me.

His mechanics were so sound that he seemed to float through a field — everything looked effortless. I had never seen such a handsome dog. He could swim all day, and actually did once when a clever hen mallard pulled the broken wing trick on him for over eight hours — pretending her wing was broken to lure Cent away from her young — as he "woof, woof, woofed" himself around a typically tranquil northern Minnesota lake.

Cent was so many wonderful things, but he was also thick. If one of my friends called him stupid, he would have been searching for his teeth, if I was within earshot. If someone said slow, I'd demo the half-Nelson on him until they took it back. Cent was neither slow nor stupid, but he was thick.

He'd swim after me when he discovered I had snuck out fishing, searching a 900-acre lake methodically to find me and then retrieve my lures or bobbers. Once Cent knew I was fishing, I was effectively finished. He'd fight coons, skunks and porcupines at the drop of a hat, and he never learned that they just weren't worth it. There was one weekend when he got into three different skunks over a 48-hour period. That used up more vinegar and tomato juice than a pickling party full of Bloody Mary drinkers. One porcupine managed to send 139 quills into his head, throat, tongue, gums, and nose before I could get him out of there and start pulling. On the way out of the field, he struck me a perfect point on a Ruffed Grouse. When I shot it, he retrieved it to hand, all the while ignoring the pain as he pushed the quills even further into his mouth.

Murphy Berkowitz was stupid. That was the dog that my friend, Thom, would tie up in the car because he'd regularly jump out the windows of the speeding vehicle. He even jumped out while tied up, which created a ferocious thumping on the side of the car while the vehicle was reducing speed from 70 mph to a stop.

Mugsy was slow. Mugsy, one of Bob Peterson's dogs, was the dog that whenever you let him out, he'd pee on your leg as you're opening the door.

Cent wasn't stupid or slow. He was thick.

One year I was hunting Ruffed Grouse. At the time I was driving a Jeep Cherokee. I had bought it brand new for $13,000 and it worked well as a grouse truck. I would keep Cent and his pal, Jäger, in the back compartment where they would lie comfortably and sleep while I drove and then rally quickly when I stopped to hunt. On this particular morning, I decided to hunt Jäger first and then use Cent for the second portion of the hunt. Off we went to prowl the grouse coverts for the delicious forest birds. As I walked away, I could hear Cent's dissatisfaction with the "woof, woof, woof" that was resounding from the truck. I knew he'd eventually settle down, but after all, I was depriving him of his best friend and of something he loved to do. Jäger made a couple of perfect points, and we got two birds over the next hour and a half. Then we returned to the now quiet vehicle to get Cent and let him get some quality time.

As I approached the vehicle, I expected Cent would be in the back sleeping, having survived his temporary rejection, but as I got closer I could see Cent on the driver's side looking intently at our approach. Upon my arrival I'd open the truck and see he had bounced his way out of the kennel, which was now in pieces. Once free to express himself, he had eaten the steering wheel and dashboard. Amazingly, there were few pieces to be found since he had truly eaten them, as would become apparent over the next several days!

Cent and I went hunting and he was predictably perfect, pointing and retrieving grouse, fueled by PVC and foam padding. Jäger slept quietly while we hunted. It would cost $1,200 to replace the dash. It cost me another $350 to get a steel-reinforced kennel so that he could never do it again.

Two months later we were back in the grouse woods and

I decided to hunt the dogs separately. I left Cent and grabbed Jäger for the first hour. I had brought a camera to catch some of her points and the last of the fall leaves. When we returned to the Cherokee, I could see from a distance that Cent was sitting in the driver's seat. As I opened the vehicle I could see that the $350 reinforced steel kennel had been tossed, turned and plied, like a strong storm tosses barns, homes and tractors. Cent had once again eaten the dashboard. He was now excited, because he knew it was his turn to go hunting. The repairs to the Jeep were another $1,200 and it cost $150 to repair the steel reinforced kennel.

I've always been grateful to Mr. Cent for teaching me an important lesson in life about automobiles. I had never known how integral dashboards are to the value of a car. If someone would have asked me what are the most expensive and valuable components to a motor vehicle, I would have guessed the engine, drive train, frame, chassis or body, but Cent Von Esterfeld had proven that on a $13,000 vehicle the dashboard was worth $1,200 or about nine percent of the total value of the vehicle, and I was now enlightened of that fact — twice over.

THE WATER WITCH

In the eighties, nineties and to this day, Bob Peterson and I have remained very good friends. This is the same Bob Peterson who had brought me Phyllis the mouse and who my mother stuck with a big bill by merely giving his boys three turtles. He and my dad had always been good friends and when Big Al passed away, Bob and I continued the close relationship they had enjoyed. We worked together, played together and most importantly, we hunted together as often as we could, wherever we could.

Long Tom Farm is our hunting camp in western Minnesota, a launching pad for exploits into the fields, lakes, swamps and potholes of western Minnesota and South Dakota. While it has good pheasant hunting, intermittent deer hunting and occasionally great duck hunting, it serves as much as a base camp as anything. The house is an old one-room schoolhouse from the 1930s, when most farms on the prairie were 160 acres and provided a living for families of six or more. With four farms to a section, it was common to have 30 or more people per square mile in the countryside. Today, the same ground has populations of less than two people per square mile and some areas just 20 percent of that. It became a farmhouse in 1954 and has a kitchen, bathroom, mud room, one bedroom, a combination dining room/living room that people sleep in and a large dormitory bunk room on the second floor with eleven beds.

The meals at Long Tom are virtually all wild game with occasionally some fresh-caught fish. The people who eat these meals are normally very hungry, tired and have usually spent the day enjoying what they love to do most — hunt. There are pranks, wisecracks, insults and pejoratives sprinkled into the experience. There is often cigar smoke, plentiful appetizers and adult beverages available, and for young people the chance to hear stories and exploits of people and dogs of the present and past as they're exchanged by the gang in attendance.

The faces at Long Tom change with frequency, as some people are there for a day because of pressing business; others may stay a weekend or a week to enjoy what may be their favorite vacation. The place is frequented by people who can't imagine that someone would actually choose to go to Hawaii or the Caribbean for a holiday; guys that can't conceive of paying good money to sit on a beach and get sand in the crack of their ass if there's a hunting season open. These are the ones who look forward to cold, early mornings,

5:00 a.m. wake-ups, in the chance the ducks might fly, deer might move or the geese may feed in the field they've scouted.

Long Tom is as much a feeling as it is a place. It's a feeling that allows a person to leave behind the troubles of the rational world, to relax, enjoy and spend good time with others of the same mind and interests. It's the feeling that allows you to let your guard down, share a joke, an extra drink, roll on the floor with your dog, throw a boot at a snorer and put all your purposeful energy into having a successful hunt. Long Tom is also the place where generations meet and interact; where they can share and enjoy each other. The ages on any given day might range from ten to 70 or even older, with representatives of each decade in between. The physicality of football doesn't allow this scope; neither does hockey or rugby, soccer or basketball. Hunting and fishing bring generations together. Today that may be their most valuable roles, in a world where we can buy our food, fish and meat, but we can't buy trust, sort character or share adventure in many places or situations in the 21st century.

Long Tom Farm is a launching pad posing as a duck camp. Its purpose is to build relationships that are frequently cross-generational and oftentimes the best friendships you'll ever have. It's one of the few places where someone can arrive burdened with problems or heartache and sort it out the way people used to do. In a world where most people have become spectators, who watch other people do something, Long Tom is a place for participants who get out and do something.

Bob and I owned the farm in Ortonville with Jim Miller and we'd frequent the place as often as possible. In 1991 we went to the farm for opening ducks and then planned to return on Sunday morning to fly to Saskatoon, Saskatchewan, for our annual trip there. Cent hunted that Saturday like the great duck dog he had become, impeccably retrieving birds for Bob and me. That Sunday morning we pass shot and he once again retrieved them to our hands. We swung by my house to drop him off as we headed to the airport to catch our plane. He looked at us very strangely as we drove away with all our hunting gear in the car, but without him.

"Boss, what are ya thinkin'?" he seemed to say. "I'm here, don't leave me!"

Bob and I had taken this trip for 12 straight years. It was our annual sojourn to Western Saskatchewan for geese and ducks. On these outings we had built friendships, become better hunters, learned the way of the wily snow goose and always had a lot of fun. It was a trip we looked forward to all year and talked about almost every time we were together. Whenever I have trouble sleeping, to this day, I transport my mind to some of the duck sloughs that Bob and I had found, and I magically fall back to sleep.

Our luggage carts were full as we wheeled them up to the ticket agent. "A big bag each, two coolers and two shotguns in hard cases to check to Saskatoon," we said in unison. "May I see your tickets please, gentlemen," the agent responded. I had the tickets and proudly presented them. The agent reviewed our paperwork, silently checked his computer, looked me square in the eye and said, "Gentlemen, these tickets were for yesterday." "What," I said, "that's impossible!" "Oh, it's quite possible," he responded. Recovering, I said, "Well, no problem, we'll go on today's flight." "Sorry, but today's flight is full, I just checked that," the agent responded. "We'll go tomorrow," I blurted. "Sold-out as well," he intoned. Reality was setting in, that we were screwed, we were not going to Saskatchewan and we were no longer hours from our favorite place — but a year.

We pushed our loaded carts over to some benches and sat silently for at least 25 minutes. We looked so forlorn that one passerby said to his daughter, "Those poor hunters must have shot their friend." Finally, the silence was broken. I said, "Bob, we're going to make some lemonade; let's pick up Jäger and Cent, head back out to the farm, and develop the plan as we go." He agreed, and we pushed our gear out to the truck.

Dale is one of the most unforgettable characters I've ever met. We've been friends for over 20 years and his hunting tentacles reach in every direction. I called him on my cell phone and told him my pitiful story. After laughing out loud in my ear, he said, "Oh, wow, that is really, really bad, but don't worry about a thing. I'll take care of everything." Dale has the habit of never saying goodbye on a phone call, he just hangs up, which is just what he did. Then minutes later he called me back. "Okay, you're all set up. I've got you two farms to hunt for upland, a set of goose decoys, a local farmer to guide you, a 60-foot trailer to live in and a guy who'll cook your breakfast every day."

"Where am I going, Dale?" I asked.

"Bottineau, North Dakota. Call me when you get there," and he hung up, just the way he does.

I explained our fate to Bob. He said, "I love lemonade," and I agreed.

As we headed west to Bottineau, we got diverted by another friend, Van Ellig, who had heard about our plight.

"Go to Mott," he said. "You just have to see how many birds there are in that area — pheasants, sharptail, Hungarian partridge," he continued. So we went to Mott. When we got into the area we were astounded at the populations. We gained access to some good ground and let Jäger and Cent loose to find birds, which they did in big numbers for about 15 minutes until they suddenly became involved with a big North Dakota skunk. The encounter lasted for a good five minutes of scratching, biting, hissing, tearing off of skin and the predictable spraying by the skunk. When it was over the "victors" were totally "skunked" and reeked beyond anything in my experience. We loaded them up in the Suburban, each in their own kennels, rolled down all the windows and headed to town to find the vet. Besides the odor issue, both dogs were scratched, wounded and bitten. As we drove, the smell was so strong that at one point I looked over at Bob and noticed that he was uncomfortably sitting as far forward in his seat and leaning as close to the windshield as he possibly could. Just as I was about to tease him about how much he'd contorted his posture just to get an extra six inches from the dogs, I realized I was doing the same thing.

As is typically the case in small rural communities, there were no small-animal vets. The large-animal vets tend to everything: cows, pigs, horses, dogs, cats and everything in between. The vet was a good sport and he dressed up the wounds and cleaned up the dogs with us the best he could. Using tomato juice, vinegar, lemon and soap we scrubbed, washed, rinsed and tried to eliminate the smell. When it was all over, we could reduce the smell, but that was it. Now we were off to Bottineau.

When we got to Bottineau, everything Dale said came true, but there was one bonus he hadn't mentioned. The guy who cooked us breakfast was a farmer who lived in the farmhouse near the trailer; he loved to talk, didn't get much company and he was also a water witch, an oil magnet and a clairvoyant. We were in for it, a full demo!

He approached us with a friendly smile; he had a non-threatening aura about him. "Let me show you around," he said. We jumped in his truck and off we went with Jäger and Cent running next to us. As soon as the door on the pickup closed, he started talking; whenever he wasn't describing the land and the good hunting spots, he was offering his life story. Not an especially fascinating story, but one as full of rejection as a red-headed stepchild's. Most of the rejection was built around his inability to convert his abilities to find water and oil the old-fashioned way. "It was a plot of the hydrologists and geologists to make finding water and oil difficult," he explained.

Unable to hide my curiosity, I asked, "Well, how do you find water and oil?" He grabbed that bait like a hungry bass, and ran like a tarpon in shallow water.

"Follow me," he said and grabbed an old car antenna. His tone changed from chatty to serious and while I would have rather gone hunting, Bob and I were soon walking across a plowed field with him leading the way, holding his right arm straight out with the antennae in front of him. We walked for about 400 yards and suddenly his arm started gyrating up and down, and the old antennae was flexing. The dogs, which were next to him, cowered at the antennae as it appeared to be aimed at them. "Right here," he yelled. "It's right here!"

Now this piece of ground didn't look any different than the other 80 acres in this field and no different than the 400 yards we'd just covered. "What's right here?" I queried.

"Water," he said with his arm continuing to move up and down like a Nazi soldier saluting.

Bob and I looked at each other quizzically.

"I don't see any water," Bob said.

"Of course not," he answered, "it's 40 feet under the ground." As we walked back to the truck he said, "Now, I'll show you oil."

At the truck he carefully put away the car antennae and now produced an old twisted coat hanger. The wire was twisted so one end of the hanger fit into the palm of his outstretched left hand and the other end fit into the palm of his right hand, which he held directly above the left hand. The balance of the wire was about 18 inches and was underneath his outstretched right arm.

We began the same type of march we had done for water, moved about 200 yards and suddenly the coat hanger remnants began to spin in a perfect circle. "It's here," he yelled.

"What's here?" I asked.

"Oil," he said.

Now this ground looked just like everything else around us and Bob said, "I don't see any oil."

"Of course not, it's 1,200 feet below us," he said. At this point we were amused, but I suggested, "it's time to go hunting," and we went back to the truck.

As we neared the truck he moved quickly to get ahead of us and grabbed a quart of 10w30 motor oil out of the pickup. He put his foot on the oil can, held out his arms with the coat hanger, just as he had carried it 10 minutes earlier. The hanger began to spin in circles once again; when he lifted his foot off the can and placed it on the ground, the spinning stopped.

Bob, Jäger, Cent and I went hunting.

The next morning he had cooked us a full breakfast and

even though neither Bob nor I eat breakfast, our good manners wouldn't let us not dig in. As the meal was winding up he took a new twist and asked, "Would you guys like to know how many birds you're going to get today?" The last thing a hunter wants to know is how many birds he's going to get; if it's zero you're totally depressed, and if it's a lot, you remove all the anticipation, but we said yes. He now held in front of his forehead a piece of string with a big heavy tractor nut strung to it. Suddenly the nut began to swing, his concentration was complete. The nut would swing back and forth 23 times and stop. "Twenty-three birds," he said, "that's how many you'll get today." We left more quietly than we had left him after the water or oil incident. This seemed disturbingly real.

We shot 16 geese that morning, went duck hunting and shot five ducks. The World Series was on TV that night and Bob wanted to see it. I went out with the dogs as the sun set and just at the last glimpse of light Mr. Cent struck a point and Jäger a back, a covey of Huns exploded and I hit a double. We had 23 birds.

That evening there was a knock on the door — it was him. He had a bunch of maps and the tractor nut. With the baseball game in the background, he never asked how many birds we'd gotten. He sat down at the kitchen table and said, "Let me show you boys something." We gathered at the table, ignoring the Yankees. "Do you guys know who Jacob Wetterling is?" he asked.

"Sure," Bob and I said, "he's the most famous kidnapping and abduction in this part of the country."

"Well, let me show you where he's buried."

Cent was asleep on the floor of the kitchen and Jäger lay

looking quizzically at the farmer and us. She had a way of lying with her paws crossed in front of her that was very feminine and distinctive. The thoughts that ran through our minds were horrific. "Oh my God, is he the abductor? He has special powers all right, what have we gotten into? Where's my gun? I'm gonna kill that Dale."

As our fears were seizing us, he spread out the maps on the table — a Minnesota highway map, a South Dakota map and a Sioux Falls city map. He held the nut to his forehead and leaned over the Minnesota map; north of St. Cloud where Wetterling was abducted it began to swing. He followed a route over the next ten minutes, the nut swinging for no apparent reason, just as it had that morning 23 times. The route switched to South Dakota and the Sioux Falls city map where, at a city park, it stopped.

"Right there," he said, "he's buried right there."

The obvious questions followed. "Who have you told? Did you call the FBI? The family?"

"They all think I'm nuts," he said dejectedly. "Do you guys think I'm nuts?" he asked. We didn't respond.

He then turned to us and said, "Do you want to know how many birds you'll get tomorrow?"

"No thanks," I said, "and I don't want to know who will win the baseball game either." It's a funny thing about lemonade — it's sweet, but it's sour.

The dogs loved that place and we enjoyed our unexpected trip and visit. On long trips Jäger had a way of sneaking into beds, which she would never do at home; Cent wouldn't even think about it. It was as if he thought he wouldn't be able to protect us all if he left his post guarding the foot of the bed.

JUST A DOG

As much as he was Jäger's pal, lover, teammate and protector, Cent did have one indiscretion during their relationship. Not too bad for a stud dog; we had him bred to a dog in New York named P.J. who had put Jäger in second place in the 1989 U.S. Open Pheasant Championship. P.J. was an outcross for us, which we needed for The Line, and a dalliance for Cent. The result was named Pinky, because P.J.'s owners always put different color ribbons on their pups to tell them apart, and this pup's ribbon was pink.

Once we had her, she became Gretchen. She grew to be big, strong, tough, quite butch. She got along well with both Jäger and Cent. Being five years younger, she was a bridge to the future. She had a very cold nose, a solid retrieve and in some ways she might have been the purest hunting dog ever. She never had a warm personality like Jäger, Abby or Chevy, but she was more of a killer than any other dog in The Line.

Cent would run farther and faster than other dogs and as a result range more. It didn't bother me, but it did bother other people sometimes. A lot of people want dogs close and under control. I really don't. I feel it's my job to stay with the dog and that the dog will find a lot more birds than I will. With more than 220 million receptors in a dog's nose (humans have five million) designed to smell 1,000 times more effectively than humans, how could I be so vain as to think I know more than the dog? The reality is that when a dog ranges a lot, they're more likely to get lost. One of my favorite places to hunt is a 3,000-acre marsh of Dale's that's a combination of low quality hay and grass and meandering wetland. It's as flat as can be, with the difference between wetlands and grasslands only 18 inches. As they cut the hay, they would create big round bales about 12 feet in diameter; wherever the bales were on this prairie was the highest point around.

When Cent would get separated from me during the hunt, his ritual was very predictable.

First he would bark. "Woof, woof, woof, woof." A loud, non-ferocious, "I'm over here, boss." This would frequently lead to reunification.

Second, if that didn't work, he would bay. "Howwwwl, howwwwl, howwwwl," to say, "no game, boss, just lettin' you know where I am. Wouldn't ya like to come get me?"

Third, if unsuccessful in that attempt, he would climb up on the top of a round bale and at first just survey the grounds, enjoying his view, admiring his athletic feat and assuming I would see his statuesque pose sooner rather than later. If I didn't show within 20 minutes or so, he would combine methods three, two and one by intermittently woofing and howling from his perch until I found him. When I'd approach, he'd stop all audio communication, look very calm and casually bound down as if to say, "Are you a little slow today, boss? I've been waiting quite a while."

Every morning we'd go running. He loved to run and so did I, and we'd run six to eight miles most days. We'd bound through parks and residential neighborhoods. I'd have one or two dogs on every run. I'd leash them to my waistband-contraption, keeping my arms free. Cent loved to run, but so did Jäger and Gretchen. Cent knew where the leashes were stored and when it was time to run he'd go pick out a leash and parade around with it in his mouth, some of it dragging on the floor or stairs, as if to say, "Time to go, boss. I'm ready for my run."

Almost every run of the thousands that we took were uneventful — just good exercise, fresh air and quality time together — but not all. Like the morning Cent, Gretchen and I were out on a residential block where there were some workmen remodeling a beautiful old home. Every day for a week, a terrier hid under the stairway and attacked us. On the Thursday, a day after the little dog had bitten Gretchen, the little rat bushwhacked us again. I broke stride for just an instant, but in that moment Gretchen had put her head under the belly of the terrier, lifted her head and flipped the little dog on its back. In her second lightning-fast move she tore the stomach out of the dog and it was dead. I was shocked! Cent was visibly surprised; Gretchen wasn't. She'd killed it and she showed no visible remorse as she shook the corpse.

"Keep going, buddy, just keep going. We've seen that dog

attack you four days in a row. It got just what it had coming," one construction worker said. Everything happened so fast, I couldn't imagine that the murder had a witness and then another guy said, "No kiddin', man, get goin'. We saw it and we'll tell the owner. You did nothin' wrong." Then as I was ready to run away with my buddy, Cent, and my murderess, Gretchen, he said, "Hell, it's just a dog."

It was then I stopped. I knew that I had to knock on that door and tell the owner what happened. To these well-intended guys it was just a dog fight and the loser had gotten what it deserved. I wanted to believe that myself for a moment, but those words "it's just a dog" snapped me back to reality.

I picked up the bloody little terrier after I tied my dogs up, carried it up to the door and rang the bell. When the owner came to the door he assumed that the dog had been hit by a car, which would have been my easy way out, but I told him the truth.

He lost his dog that day, but I lost something, too. I lost the total confidence and complete certainty that my dog Gretchen would never again act that way. I now knew how violent she could be, how quickly it could happen and how tragically it could end. The same trait that I had seen her display when dispatching coons, skunks, possums and porcupines had now shown itself in her attack on a little terrier.

We took her to the vet and ran tests to see if there was something physical that had bolted this behavior. And she had in fact developed a thyroid condition called Cushing's disease that had altered her body chemistry and made her more aggressive. Most dogs affected are eight years or older; the symptoms include increased water intake and urination, hair loss and skin problems, pot belly, energy loss, and behavior problems such as irritability, biting and snapping. She took medication for the rest of her life, and she never killed another dog. Now there were some skunks, coons, possums, and porcupines that didn't survive, but she never killed another dog and she was never anything but friendly with people.

JÄGER GETS SICK

She lay on her dog bed shivering and docile. Jäger was sick or injured, we didn't know which. She had trouble standing and had lost the sparkle in her eyes. After a day of watching her suffer, it was off to the vet. He too was perplexed, as he'd never seen these symptoms under these circumstances. We began to research, checking journals and papers for clues as to what could be wrong with the developing champion. Cent lay beside her, licking her head and snuggling with her to keep her warm. She liked his attention and body heat. They were now beyond pals, they were partners in every way and he shared her misery.

We had a breakthrough: a recently published paper about a disease that had first been found in Lyme, Connecticut, carried by deer ticks. The disease could affect dogs or humans. It begins with the tick bite, which then creates a red circle followed days later by the flu-like symptoms Jäger was demonstrating — the joint pain, trembling and fever. The disease then goes dormant and returns for another bout in about six months; then there is a frequently fatal rebound after about two years, with a continuing deterioration over the two-year period. The disease existed in the East, but there was no indication that it had spread to the Midwest, which is why the vet didn't recognize it. The vet, John Bailey, whose life would weave in and out of ours for over 30 years, read the research and said, "By God, this just might be it!"

The antidote was quite simple: a course of Tetracycline, and the killing cycle would be defeated. Within days, Jäger was one-hundred percent. This was the early nineties and it was the first case of Lyme disease diagnosed west of Ohio. We later figured that the ticks hitchhiked on a shipment of birds bought in the east. Soon the disease spread all over the country and by now, people know what to watch for. Before the disease became ubiquitous, countless dogs and many people perished from it. We learned that research and study are essential ingredients when it comes to dogs and disease — a lesson that would serve us well in the future.

MICH

Over the last 25 years Bruce Wohlrabe has been one of my best friends and a huge asset to The Line. Shortly after his divorce he also lost his black Lab, who had been his pal, hunting partner and commiserator. He arrived at the club one day missing his daughters and his home, so he was a prime prospect for a pup. The first Jäger-Cent litter was only seven weeks old, and Jäger was a predictably doting mother. Cent was a photogenic proud father, but he wasn't immersed in the pup-raising process. The long-awaited litter sold briskly at the premium price of $1,000 per pup, a price that most people didn't think was possible at the time.

When Bruce arrived, he had two attractive girls with him and gave the unmistakable impression he was dating them both at the same time — something few people could pull off, though Bruce was on that short list. I ran into the three of them as they were enjoying a Michelob Light and immediately the conversation shifted to puppies and the litter out at the kennels. The girls wanted to see the puppies in the worst way, but Bruce was a little cool on the idea of shorthairs, as he'd been a Lab guy all his life.

"Oh, you know they won't hunt ducks with me," Bruce insisted.

"Bruce, they'll hunt ducks, I'm tellin' ya. Look at Cent, he hunts ducks all day, you know that," I responded.

"Come on, Bruce, let's see the puppies," the girls said, and they dragged him out the door. The three of them piled into the front seat of his pick-up truck and drove a quarter-mile to the kennel. I followed.

The weather was sunny and the temperature 75 degrees Fahrenheit. There was little wind and there may not have been a prettier place to be that day than the club. Lilacs were still out and the honeysuckle was in bloom; the crops along the road were about knee-high and the corn and sorghum were flourishing. They would make excellent hunting cover in only a couple of months.

When I arrived, Bruce said, "I want to see if they'll even go in the water. I know they won't swim, but will they even go in the water?" He had a belligerent tone in his voice, so I said, "Of course they'll go in the water. What do you think?" I really had no idea, but if genetics are the key to puppies, I was blindly confident in my statement.

"Oh, are they cute!" the girls said simultaneously when they saw Jäger's nine pups. Because some were already sold, I tried to draw their attention to a mid-sized male that was still available. He looked unspectacular when compared to the dominating brown behemoths that roamed the same kennel. His face had a decisive blaze of white running down his nose that upset the symmetry of his face. His ticking was without pattern, and he was probably the most unprepossessing of any dog in that litter or in any of Jäger and Cent's future litters. I grabbed him and presented him to the girls who loved him immediately. Despite his visual shortcomings, he was cute, very healthy and fearless.

We walked down to the dog pond while the puppy toddled or was carried along, catching everyone's eyes on the way.

"Don't worry, Bruce, he'll go in," I said. "And if he does, you're buying him, deal?"

Bruce nodded, the girls cooed and now it was up to the pup. If he swam, he was riding home with Bruce and his two attractive dates in the already crowded front seat of the Chevy pick-up.

All questions were resolved in seconds as the pup saw the water, got a running start and plunged in quickly, shifting to a dog paddle and then fetching a stick Bruce threw him. When he returned to shore it was Bruce who grabbed him, not the girls, and he held him up as proud as if he were an Academy Award. The girls cheered.

"What should we name him?" they asked, and Bruce calmly said, "Mich," holding up his beer bottle to confirm the spelling; not Mick or Mickey, but *Mich*, M-I-C-H, as in Michelob.

The girls approved and Bruce wrote a check on the spot. They all piled into the front seat of the Chevy pick-up: Bruce, his two dates and Mich. At only seven weeks he was the first pup to go home out of that litter. We usually send them at eight weeks, but this was an exception — and Mich would be an exception his entire life.

I never followed Mich the way I should have because we had some other great performers from that litter and I was enamored with them. At the time, of course, Jäger was in her prime and Cent in his, and Gretchen had arrived, so the probability of something coming along to upset their pace never occurred to me.

Whenever I'd see Bruce or talk to him, he'd sing the praises of the "blazed" dog — how quick he learned (*Jäger*, I'd think), how strong he was (*Cent*, I'd think) — but I really never spent much time monitoring his advancement. In his second year, Bruce asked me if I'd compete him in a tournament and I declined, because my schedule was too full with Jäger, Cent and my partner's Labs. Bruce was stung, but still my pal.

His faith in Mich never wavered and without me knowing it, he had invested a lot of money into the dog with Terry Holzinger, the great dog trainer. Again without me realizing it, he had entered Mich with Terry and his old friend, Tim Tucker — who was a crack shot — in the U.S. Open Pheasant Championship, the nation's largest tournament and one I expected to win. During the auction of competing teams — the Calcutta — on the night before the tournament began, I left the room briefly and this gave Bruce the chance to buy his Mich run very economically; no one had heard of Mich or Tucker, so no bids of any size surfaced from the field, while runs involving myself and Jäger or Cent went for over $300. When I returned to the auction, no one said a word about what I'd missed. On the last day of the four-day event, Mich would go out with Terry and Tim and win the U.S. Open, knocking his mother Jäger into second place and Cent to fifth. Bruce had pocketed over $6,000 on his entry with the two-year-old and I had been served crow for dinner. From that moment on, I viewed Mich differently, and I never missed a chance to compete behind him because of the excitement he'd generate.

He was still "blazed," but he had grown into a handsome, athletic, finely toned, mid-sized dog; he had perfect conformation, making his strides effortless even in the thickest cover. His nose was certain, and while it was a hot nose, he had a cold quality that allowed him to track very well. His homeliness had transformed into athletic vigor; his head blazed, but held high.

When the Twins won the World Series in game seven at home, Bruce and I had just gone hunting out west with Jäger, Cent, Gretchen and Mich. I had tickets to the game and invited Bruce to go. We watched Jack Morris pitch ten innings and keep the Braves scoreless. When the Twins won, we went to celebrate along with the rest of the city. That night Bruce said to me, "Mich should be your dog; you'll compete him, breed him and make him the best he can be. I'll sign the papers over to you, but he continues to live with me and I'll never have to buy another dog again. What do you say?"

I shook his hand and closed the deal on the spot. With that The Line now had its second great male and one who could tournament hunt like few other dogs in history.

As Mich would always surprise us, he also surprised other people. Bruce went off to the Great Delta Marsh duck hunting the next fall. In spite of years of duck hunting, it was his first trip to the Delta Marsh in Manitoba, Canada. This is the storied marsh of Jimmy Robinson, the famous writer of *Sports Afield*, whose camp had hosted Ted Williams in his prime. Clark Gable was a regular, along with countless lesser stars, numerous captains of industry and accomplished athletes. This is Lab country, though you might see the occasional Chesapeake. Manitoba gets cold and the water is big and daunting. When you hunt the Delta Marsh, you go out in the morning and stay out all day, eating lunch in the field. Photos of the famous line the walls in the buildings, and each shot seems to shout, "This is the hunting capital of the world!"

Bruce brought Mich to Jimmy Robinson's camp. From the moment he arrived, a whisper arose as guides eyeballed the shorthair dog curiously, while other guests wrinkled noses and foreheads over Bruce and Mich's presence.

The amiable Bruce bludgeoned through looks, sneers and innuendoes, and over several drinks found at least some civility in the camp. At breakfast the next morning, the head guide came to find Bruce.

"Mr. Wohlrabe, sir," he said stiffly. "I need to talk to you."

"Go ahead," Bruce said, never a formal guy.

"Alone."

They stepped into an entryway and the guide said, "Sir, you can't take your dog into the marsh. It is the place of only Labradors and Chesapeakes, water dogs with thick, oily coats that can withstand the water for hours, if necessary. Your dog will likely perish out there and we cannot be responsible. I have a kennel where it can be kept during the day."

The guide seemed to be finished, so Bruce spoke. "This dog goes with me everywhere. I've had him since he was seven weeks old. He rides with me in the front seat of my truck, summer or winter," he said. "He hunts ducks, geese, pheasant or anything I ask, including fur. He's my best friend, he coached me through my divorce, helped me rebuild a business, helped me attract a new wife and won the national championship last year. Now, he's goin' where I'm goin', and I'm goin' huntin'."

"Sir," the head guide implored. "Sir, we do not allow Dalmatians on the Delta Marsh!"

Needless to say, Mich went hunting that day and every day for the rest of their stay. He retrieved ducks and swam and had a grand old time keeping up with the Labs and Chesapeakes. Every day on their return, the head guide would look at Bruce's boat as it motored in off the huge marsh, to see if the "damned Dalmatian" had made it back. Bruce suppressed the urge to tell the codger that Mich was a German shorthair pointer and one of the best that ever lived. As Mich aged and Bruce started a new family, his daughters would dress the dog up with crowns and capes and pose him as "Super Dog" and other characters. He willingly submitted to their wishes, even on Halloween, when it really got humiliating for the champion.

GRETCHEN

By three years of age, Gretchen had become the best all around dog of the pack — and probably the best in The Line — when it came to hunting. At 65 pounds, Gretchen was a large female with excellent conformation and phenomenal strength. She had also become a very good tournament dog, winning state titles and always showing well, especially in bad weather. Her cold nose and ability to sort smells by shifting her head position gave her an edge in bad weather. She and Jäger got along very well as did she with her father, Cent.

For years I would take at least one, sometimes two, fishing trips to Saskatchewan each summer, heading off for Big Northerns, Walleyes, Lake Trout and Grayling. In the process I became good friends with my fishing guide, Ed Morretto, a British Columbia native. Ed loved to fish, but he also loved to hunt, and when he could, he spent his falls in Minnesota so we could hunt as much as possible. He and I and the dogs — Jäger, Cent and Gretty — would pack up and head to Long Tom where we'd hunt virtually every waking hour.

When the Halloween Storm of '91 hit us, Ed and I rambled west into the brunt of the storm, believing it would drive the northern flight right to us. The normally three-hour drive took us seven hours. We drove in whiteout conditions through a freak storm that dropped rain first, which soon became ice, and then covered the ice in 19 inches of wind-whipped snow. Only fools and duck hunters would dare venture out in this tempest. We would frequently take turns walking in front of the truck to make sure we were still on the road, while the other drove slowly behind the walking man. When it cleared enough that we could see 40 or 50 yards, the walker jumped back in and we'd drive awhile. It was some of the roughest conditions I've ever seen, being Minnesotan and a Canadian, we weathered it as if it were routine. When we finally made it out to the farm, the Northern flight had over-flown us, the lake was frozen solid and our trip was for nothing. To make matters worse, some poachers had snuck onto the farm, used my equipment, and abandoned the decoys to the elements. They were now scattered all over the lake and hopelessly frozen in. Due to the deep snow, the poachers lodged their truck up on a huge rock leaving the vehicle hopelessly stuck at a 45 degree angle. Needless to say, their escape was dashed; they had to walk out of the blizzard.

As the weather calmed down two days later, Ed and I

went pheasant hunting with the gang. It was just a joy to hunt these three dogs — all in their prime — on native birds, which, due to the extended prairie drought, were in high numbers. Gretchen could knock down cover and dig into the thick stuff as adeptly as Cent. And that's how she got in trouble on the Sunday morning.

It started with some barking and then it launched into a full scale battle. Gretchen and the coon were going at it. I yelled "coon fight" to Ed and, like the veterans we were, we ran to the sounds of the skirmish. She was fully engaged and I feared that Cent or Jäger would suddenly appear out of nowhere to join the fray, as would have been typical. I moved into the fight with my shotgun at the ready.

"Ed, stay here and don't let Cent or Jäger into the fight. I'm going to shoot the coon."

"Okay," he yelled back.

I approached the combatants and saw it was a big coon. My plan was to grab Gretchen, hold her with one arm, then stick the barrel of my shotgun into the coon and shoot it. I moved in, grabbed Gretty, stuck the barrel into the coon. As I did, Gretchen lunged toward the coon. I was in calf-deep water now and off balance. I pulled the trigger and blood, mud and water flew everywhere. Gretchen collapsed in the mire, covered with blood and not moving.

"Ed, I've shot my dog! Ed, Ed, I've shot Gretchen!"

I fell to my knees and cradled her in my arms.

"Oh, Gretchen. Oh, Gretchen. I didn't mean to. I'm so sorry."

Then her eyes opened and I saw she was alive. Her head rolled and she looked dazed, but she was alive. Then she struggled to stand and jumped out of my grasp. I grabbed her again to examine her and she didn't have a single wound. I realized later that when I pushed the muzzle into the coon, the concussion of the shell all went out the porting, and that's what knocked her out. The blood belonged to the coon. Within minutes we were all hunting again and Gretchen was none the worse for wear. She was tough.

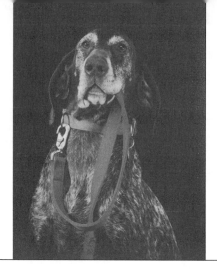

MR. CENT
GOES EXPLORING

Nineteen ninety-two was the driest year in a three-year drought. In the Midwest, even the old, deep sloughs were dry. In the perpetual optimism that only farmers and outdoorsmen seem to share, we went out to Long Tom Farm to plant trees, hoping against hope that they would survive the summer. As the day went on, it got hotter and hotter and the winds rose to 50 miles per hour. We intended to plant 1,200 trees that day, and our pace was set by my friend Bruce, a landscaper and tree-planting expert. While Jäger lay in the field near us laborers and Mich relaxed by the truck, Cent needed to go exploring. He just couldn't help it. He had wandered about a quarter of a mile west to what we call the "rock slough," a small wetland that was now dry and filled with rocks and cattails. The strong winds were blowing right at us from the rock slough that Cent was exploring.

As we dug a three-feet-deep hole for a four-foot spruce, we began to hear barking in the distance. The wind carried the sound to us, so Cent sounded much closer than he was. To me, the barking was a clear indication something was up, and it would have rallied Jäger, Gretchen and Mich, but they were sound asleep. I suspected that the barking meant Cent had found a coon or skunk, a very probable scenario because coons and skunks love rock piles. I was too tired to go get him, and due to the wind, he'd never hear me call him off whatever he was up to, so he was on his own.

Several minutes later it became very clear what he had found. When a skunk first sprays, it doesn't smell like the foul odor we all associate with skunks; in actuality, at first, it smells like a highly concentrated dose of pepper. It's not necessarily even offensive in those first few minutes, but soon the putrid smell we all associate with skunks kicks in.

"Wow," Bruce said laughing, "he sure got him. This is your lucky day."

I merely shook my head, smiled lamely and went on with my work thinking about how Cent's eyes must be burning, his mouth befouled and his sensitive nose deeply insulted by the skunk's action.

Ten minutes later Bruce started to laugh.

I looked up and said, "What's up?"

He pointed west and I turned; coming at me was Cent Von Esterfeld, moving with a regal gait across the quarter-mile field with a pride reminiscent of a military hero receiving a commendation. His head was high, his stride confident, his posture perfect — and from his mouth hung a dead skunk that he carried as if it were the King's Golden Goose.

His objective, naturally, was to deliver it to me to hand, presenting this valuable prize to the boss. Bruce's laughter wasn't at Cent; it was all at my expense. I was the one who had to take it out of his mouth. Upon his arrival he paraded to my side and sat, presenting his prize, at which point I took it out of his mouth with the command "mein." I then said, "Gut hund, Cent" and patted his head. He swelled with pride and sauntered off to start his next adventure, reeking of skunk. I promptly threw the deceased into a deep tree hole, put a spruce on top of it and filled in the hole. We continued our back-breaking work, knowing it would pay off in the future.

Then Bruce started in again with his "Oh, brother" type comments and snide grin, and I looked in the direction he was pointing. There stood His Majesty, Cent Von Esterfeld, looking strong and regal, if perhaps a bit disheveled, as he was covered with dirt on his legs, head, paws and front quarters, with the freshly dug-up stinky, filthy skunk corpse in his mouth. His expression said it all — "Hey, boss, did you lose something?" was written all over his face. He pranced to my side and re-presented the highly fragrant skunk once again.

At this point it was my honor to say, "Mein, Cent. Danke. Du bist ein gute hund," and take the mammal from his mouth. Out of his sight we put the corpse in an even deeper hole and planted a tree on top of it. By fall the scorching summer had killed all the trees we labored to plant that day, except one that seemed to have a little something extra to tide it through the scorching hot drought. Why, Cent even had a way of affecting the landscape.

SADIE

Sadie was a member of Jäger and Cent's second litter, making her a full sister to Mich, though not a littermate. Attractive, brave and confident, she shined among a bunch of outstanding pups. When the guy who had purchased her came to pick her up, it was the first time the two ever saw each other. He had purchased her over the telephone, sight unseen. He had third-pick female and asked that we choose for him, which we were glad to do. He was burly and unkempt, introduced himself and coldly asked, "Well, where is she?"

He grabbed her by the nape of the neck, quite tightly, and she whined a bit with pain. He held her awkwardly, but he seemed to warm to her the way people do with pups. As he was leaving, he asked about our guarantee which states: "If for any reason you're not pleased with your pup or dog, we'll take it back and replace it with another dog."

We didn't hear from him again for 15 months, and then we got the phone call. "I'm bringing my dog back. I'm not happy with her. Are you gonna honor your guarantee?" he asked.

"Of course we'll honor it," we said.

"I'll be there at two," he said, and he hung up.

He drove up in an old, dirty pickup truck, not the same truck he drove away in 15 months earlier, and he was even rougher looking than when I had seen him last. Sadie was riding in the bed of the pickup, not in a kennel or box, just sliding around back there. When he snapped, "Sadie, get down," she physically cowered. It was obvious she feared his voice. The minute I saw that, I realized that this may not be a household where I wanted to place another young pup, which is what our guarantee would require. I hurried into the kennel hoping to find a female voice quickly, and sure enough the kennel girl, Jeanne, was there.

"Come with me, please," I asked. "We need to hurry. There's a dog I need you to talk to." She smiled and followed quickly.

On the way to his truck I said, "I need you to say in a loud firm voice, 'Sadie, get down,' okay?" She nodded. As we closed in on the two of them, Jeanne said, "Sadie, get down," Sadie immediately complied without any cowering or fear. Then Jeanne played with Sadie and threw some dummies, which Sadie retrieved perfectly. "What's wrong in your opinion?" I asked the man.

"She's just a scaredy cat, too soft. She just hasn't got it."

"How long has it been this way?"

"About six months now. She was doing good, but then I took her to South Dakota and it just got worse and worse until she was finally walking behind me. My friends sure had a good time making fun of me. I kept pushing her out in front of me, but she wouldn't go. Now I just can't even stand to be around her, she's so timid."

"How many hunters were there?" I asked.

"About 20 altogether," he said.

Then suddenly I turned and loudly said, "Sadie, get down." She immediately cowered to my male voice.

"Where do you have the pups for me to choose from?"

"I don't," I said.

He looked at me with a mean eye. "Hold it," he said. "I bought this dog because of the guarantee! You promised me that if things didn't work out, I could get another dog!" he yelled.

"I'm going to give you your money back instead," I interrupted.

"Well, I guess that would be okay, too."

I quickly counted out his cash, paid him and said goodbye.

When we had Sadie x-rayed, just as I suspected we found BBs in her from an accident about six months previously. This guy and his buddies had shot the dog and probably didn't even know they had done it. On an action-filled Dakota hunt with 20 guys and lots of dogs, such an accident can go unnoticed, but obviously it frightens a young pup who should never be in such a confusing situation in the first place. As we left the vet's office, I conducted the last of the necessary experiments, even though I feared it would break my heart. As we walked back to my truck I raised my right hand down swiftly toward her as if to strike her. She cowered completely;

it was obvious she had been struck in this manner many times. I swore then and there we would find her a home where she would never fear a male voice or live with the threat of a beating again.

By giving him his money back, I didn't have to worry about what would happen to the next poor pup that ended up in that house. I cut off our relationship and his link to The Line. Within weeks, Sadie's confidence was back and her hunt desire fully restored. Within months her fear of men was unnoticeable in almost all situations and her personality was back. She was the brave, attractive, confident pup we said goodbye to all those months ago.

For all reputable breeders, the question of placement always looms large as each litter develops regardless of the particular breeds. There is probably no one who has been in the business for any meaningful period of time who hasn't had to deal with the gut-wrenching decision to place a pup with a person they don't feel good about. To look someone in the eye and tell them, "You're a jerk and I won't sell one of my pups to you," is a rarely expressed combination of words. It is not, however, a rarely felt sentiment. Generally, I believe that people who whine, bitch or complain about one thing are likely to whine, bitch and complain about other things. I don't care if it's the weather, their truck dealer, their last dog trainer, whatever the topic — if the person is fundamentally negative, they're likely to be negative about everything, including an innocent puppy.

When a dealer sells a pool table to someone for their rec room, they don't really care if they like the customer or not. After all, they don't care about the pool table once it's delivered, and they don't ever need to see the person again, as long as they get paid. They really don't care if the guy is a jerk. The same applies to most products and even services. When it comes to dogs and puppies, this rule just doesn't hold up because you know that the little living, breathing, sensitive being you've struggled to perfect as best you can will have to live with the whining, bitching complainer for the rest of its life — 10, 12 or 15 years after you've cashed the check and forgotten what you spent it on.

The result is that when we come across what we perceive to be "the jerk," we have several little tricks that work pretty well to keep away from a mismatch. There are days to show dogs and there are days to not show dogs. Whether it's a six-month-old started dog or a four-year-old finished dog, it's really tough or nigh onto impossible to make it look good on a hot, humid summer day. When the temperature soars to over 80 degrees Fahrenheit, most dogs will only hold up for 10 to 15 minutes. In heat, as they tire, dogs tend to create frothy foam in the mouths that coats their tongues and affects their ability to smell. This, along with rapid breathing, can reduce a dog's effectiveness dramatically. Beyond these problems, in the summer the grasses are full of chlorophyll, which emit smells of their own, and the tall grasses of summer block wind and breezes, causing less scent in general to circulate. To make matters worse, if you use pigeons for your demonstrations, dogs are often reluctant to retrieve on hot, humid days because their feathers are soft, and a tired, foamy-mouthed dog can get finicky under those conditions. These circumstances can help a breeder scare off a creep.

I leaned on these tricks when such a character took a liking to our Jäger-Cent breeding. When he called me and said he'd like to come look at my dogs, I audibly groaned over the phone, but rather than say, "I'd never sell a dog to you, you're a jerk," I agreed to a demo. He drove all the way from Milwaukee to see our now one-and-a-half-year-old Sadie. I had scheduled the meeting for 2:30 in the afternoon, the time when I thought the heat would be at its highest. I took Sadie out and worked her in the heat from 12:30 to 1:30 p.m., thoroughly exhausting her, and when I set up the demo I used pigeons only, knowing it would weaken her retrieves. When he arrived, I said, "Hi, Dave. Hope you had a good trip," to which he responded, "How could I have a good trip when the first part was full of construction and the last part was driving through the Twin Cities with all the shitty drivers you have in Minnesota. Where is the little bitch anyway?"

I cringed at his edge. I hate it when dog people call female dogs bitches. Most people who do it want to convey a crusty air of experience that makes them seem professional. They want to harken back to an era of the early 20th century when people did talk that way, but today most breeders have discovered they can describe a female without using that word.

"Well, let me get her out and take a look. She's a willing rascal," I said.

As I let her out of her kennel, I was praying she was tired and unwilling enough to get this creep back in his car and heading east, right back to Wisconsin. From the minute she hit the ground, he got started.

"Wow, she's puny. I thought she was bigger than that. Isn't her head too big for her body? Why doesn't she have more white on her? Is that her natural gait? She looks like she's bowlegged."

I never said a word, only hoping to get this session over with quickly. She began to run bigger than I had hoped, covering ground really well.

"Slow down and miss the scent," I was saying to myself as she struck a point.

"Nuts!" I whispered to myself.

"Hey, that was pretty nice for a hot day," Dave said.

When the bird rose I shot it, hoping she'd miss the retrieve — she didn't. It was perfect and right to hand. I then went to set another bird in the launcher, but decided this demo was going too well, so I set the launcher, but didn't put a pigeon in it. Bird launchers are training devices that are spring loaded and remote controlled. When the remote releases the spring, the bird is launched into the air. While an unloaded launcher may have some bird odor, it is minimal compared to when it holds a bird. Sure enough she didn't strike point and he was unmerciful.

"What's with this bitch? She can't find a bird worth nothin'. Bill, if this is the best you've got, I'm surprised you've been able to stay in business."

"Would you like to see more?" I asked.

"Hell, no! This was a waste of my time. That dog couldn't catch a cold, Bill. If I were you, I wouldn't waste my time on her." He got in his truck and left. Sadie and I rolled in the grass and played for 20 minutes after he left.

Two years later, he was banned for life from tournament hunting for cheating. A woman who suspected his stunts had hidden in a field of tall grass long before sunrise, hoping to catch him on videotape. Sure enough, right on cue along he came and under cover of darkness he carefully broke the legs of some birds and placed them on the outside edge of the field he was going to hunt during the competition. By placing the birds inbounds, but in outside remote spots, it was unlikely anyone else would find them, and his illicit little plot would go undetected. With the proof on videotape, this scoundrel was abolished for good.

As for Sadie, several weeks after Dave left, on a cool and breezy day, in front of a really nice guy with two kids and a lovely wife, she put on a demo that would stop the heart of any hunter. Striking points and making retrieves on game birds that would cause the viewer to say "I'll take her!" She lived in that happy house for over 12 years, and when she finally expired, she had four people who wept over her grave — and not once in those 12 years did anyone ever call her "bitch."

ICE

Jim and Ann Miller have been friends and partners of mine since the mid-seventies. Jim and I had worked together in my early days in the ad business. Ann has always been a social spitfire, with a sparkle in her eye and a clever tongue; you never know what she might say next, or whether it might be seasoned with a profanity to catch her audience off guard. We had bought Long Tom Farm together in 1979 along with the Petersons, and the Millers would be very important participants in the development of The Line. They had also developed a line of their own that included Andy, Ellie and Tim Miller — bright and likeable kids I had watched grow up.

Andy Miller and I have hunted together since he was 12 years old. By the time he became a young physician, he had also become a good hunter and a very good dog man. One cold day the temperature was about 20 degrees Fahrenheit as we walked for pheasants along the shallow lake where the birds were using the cover of the shoreline as their refuge. We had Cent, Gretchen and Jäger on the ground, and they were putting on a clinic as they tore through the tough cover with Andy and me hanging right with them.

The lake was frozen, and because of the wind direction, Cent figured out the best place for scenting was on the frozen lake itself, where the wind was sending the scent from the shoreline. He slipped and slid on the slick ice — a dog's pads and nails can't cling to the smooth surface. Cent struck point and we raised a rooster which exploded out of the cover toward the lake. We dropped the bird about 40 yards out on the lake. Cent sped after the rooster to make the retrieve. As he was returning on the slippery surface with the bird in his mouth, he fell through. The sound of breaking ice was unmistakable, followed by his thrashing and splashing. He tried to crawl his way out but at first the ice broke as he put his paw on it and then he couldn't gain a hold because of the slickness. I turned to Andy and said, "Go as fast as you can to the truck and drive it out here. Keep the heat on high. I'm gonna be mighty cold when I come out of here."

He knew exactly what I had to do and knew that I had about 20 minutes to break a water path through the ice to save Cent. Hypothermia sets in by then and doesn't release its grip easily. I was sure the water wasn't over my head. Andy ran to the truck. I charged onto the ice. As I moved out I knew at some point it would break and I would fall in. At about 20 yards out, I fell through, and the water was up to my waist so I could use my upper body to kip up on the ice and break it as I inched my way to Cent. He was still trying to break or claw his way out, but it wasn't working. He made no progress. I was breaking ice with the weight of my body and the good news was it was getting easier, not more difficult. Two feet at a time I broke the ice and moved toward Cent. I was very cold. The water had soaked me through, but I just kept breaking ice. Then I was within reach. I lurched up for the last distance that separated us, and as I did, Cent lunged for me and we were reunited. I pulled, he scrambled and then swam right out. I turned and began to move back toward shore, hoping now that Andy wasn't far away with the truck. When Cent reached the spot where I had fallen through, he realized he didn't have the pheasant. He turned and swam back past me to pick it up. At this point, I was only concerned with getting myself out, but when I realized what he had done, I felt warm on the inside.

We both emerged from the icy water at about the same time and I immediately started tearing off my boots and clothes, counting on Andy's imminent arrival with the truck. I heard the engine as I was getting my pants off and he drove right up next to me with the heater blasting. Andy was still catching his breath from the rough run across the picked cornfield, but he had done exactly what I needed, exactly when I needed it done. Within 15 minutes I was warmed up; I changed clothes and we were back hunting.

JÄGER'S OCTOBER

Jäger had proven herself in so many ways by five years old. Due to her abilities, she had won numerous tournaments and she had helped develop the leapfrog method of play where the dog bounces back and forth between two hunters, being handled by either person equally as the case requires. She had been a great mother to two litters, caring for pups with devotion. She had proven to be a pal and running mate, and when Merry died, promoted herself to leader of the pack.

I always looked forward to the weekend in October when Bruce and I would host a group of friends at Long Tom Farm in Ortonville and at our duck club, NYROCA. We hunted pheasant, partridge and ducks and always had a good time in the process. Usually ten or 12 guys were in attendance, some experienced, some not, this being the only weekend most would hunt all year. NYROCA had been a private membership club since the 1900s. Located on a beautiful point in western Minnesota, in dry years it was a magnet for migrating waterfowl. The club had 14 members and a good facility for feeding and sleeping a group. Despite my membership, I rarely stayed there, because the club had a rule against having dogs in the buildings, which I never understood at a hunting camp, but observed out of respect.

The group met up at Long Tom on a Sunday afternoon, as we had for the previous five years, with guys arriving in twos and threes ready to hunt, some upland. I knew that an area we called the "one-sixty" was carrying a lot of Hungarian partridge and pheasants, so I suggested we start our hunting there. As we pulled into the area, the 12 or 13 guys in five different vehicles began to unload, grab guns and vests and prepared to hunt, loading up the shotguns. Then we let out, Jäger, Cent, Gretchen and Mich; four of the best would be on the ground that afternoon. There were light winds, blue skies and it was 50 degrees Fahrenheit; it was a perfect day to walk and chase birds.

Almost immediately the dogs locked onto point, Jäger locating the birds first and the others honoring her point. I did my best to line up the far-too-large group, which we had intended to divide into four groups with one dog each, but we changed our plan in response to the dogs' lead. When the partridge first rose, I sensed there would be a covey, and most certainly there was. Over 20 low-flying Hungarian Partridge exploded into the sky and hunters began to fire. Sensing the danger of the situation, I began to yell, "Don't shoot the dogs! Don't shoot the dogs!"

The Huns were flying so low as to alarm me. As I yelled the second time, I saw the shot rip into Jäger's head and watched with horror as she yelped a high-pitched scream and then raced away from the whole grisly scene, heading into a cattail slough to escape her pain and confusion. As she raced I could see the blood covering her head, and no bidding by me could stop her exit. The other dogs began the process of retrieving the fallen birds, but that wasn't my concern. Jäger was my concern.

Within seconds Al, one of the guys, said, "I did it, I did it. I shot the dog." His sadness was palpable. He was on the trip in part to get away for a little while from the reality of his wife's cancer, which was slowly killing her.

I raced after Jäger, calling as I ran into the dry cattails. There was no sign after a half-hour search. Then on the road a quarter mile away, a car stopped and someone was waving at me. I moved quickly toward the car, and as I got closer, I could see Jäger and the car's owner who was yelling, "It's hurt, but alive!"

Her head was dirty and matted with fresh blood. She didn't exhibit the clarity she usually possessed. She had always looked you in the eye, a rare quality in dogs that makes them seem smart and in the game. It was when I was looking for that "Jäger looking you in the eye" response that I realized her eye had been shot out. She was slowly sinking into shock, but at least I had her now and she wasn't lapsing into shock in some cattails, never to be seen again.

Al and I left the rest of the hunting group and raced off to a vet over 40 minutes away. He was a large-animal vet, but very competent and luckily opened for us on a Sunday. His summation was brief: "She'll probably live; she had 23 pellets in her head and it wasn't advisable to remove them. Three pellets had hit her left eye; one was firmly embedded and maybe a specialist could do something, but probably not. She is certainly blind in that eye, at least for now." Then he added a few more words: "I don't know if she'll ever hunt again."

As we drove back to the farm with Jäger asleep in the back seat, Al assured me he'd cover all the vet bills, medications and expenses. He was in the insurance business and knew that these things can add up. I thanked him and acknowledged that I knew he wasn't trying to shoot the dog.

Jäger rested the balance of the day and evening. At that time I had to call Kath and tell her what had happened to her best little friend Jäger. On that call we both broke up; some tears seemed to help.

It was 1991, and for over a year Jäger would visit vets and specialists. She would have to wear a "party hat," as we called it, a plastic cone over her head to keep her from scratching the eye. She couldn't hunt, but she did exercise with me and maintain her conditioning. It was a great year for Cent who had always been Jäger's runner-up. He would now win tournaments and collect trophies like he never had before, and Gretchen grew and developed in Jäger's absence, as well. As good as they were, though, I missed the rare, sheer quickness and intelligence that Jäger brought to the field, the excitement that makes your feet light even when you're exhausted because you always know that with her there anything was possible. She just made things happen.

Months later I numbly read a letter from Al. It read: "It seems like the bills just keep coming, but my responsibility is up at $500. So here's a check that brings me to $500. That's all I can do. — Al." The total costs ran over $3,500, not including all the medications and vet trips and specialist trips, and I lost my favorite dog. He and I never talked again. I wasn't so much angry as disappointed.

Fifteen months after the accident, the vet said Jäger could try to hunt if I wanted. "I don't know if she will hunt. There may be too much association with the pain and injury. She might be gun shy. I just don't know. The eye isn't going to come back, though. She'll remain blind, but there's no reason to baby her, so let 'er fly and see how it goes."

I was at the starting line of the Minnesota State Pheasant Championship in a Top Gun run — singles, just me and Jäger. It felt like business as usual and she seemed excited to be back in the field after 15 months. She looked me in the eye the way she always had, though one eye was very milky. I released her at the gate and the run began. She raced into the field as if no time had passed, as if 23 pellets had never entered her head, as if she'd never worn a "party hat" or needed eye drops every day. She moved with the sweet quickness she had always possessed. The only difference was that now she would occasionally rise up on her rear legs and pitch her head to her good eye to see where I was. She could still hunt.

That April a one-eyed dog named Jäger and I would win the U.S. Open Pheasant Championship, Top Gun Division. Her final winning retrieve was over a deep stream, on a blind retrieve. She bounded up and down the stream's steep walls and the half-blind dog had no trouble with the blind retrieve. I retired her from competition that afternoon.

As they aged together, Cent would always walk, run or stay on Jäger's left. He somehow knew that it was her vulnerable side.

MR. CENT FIGHTS
FOR HIS LIFE

We were in a cattail slough choked with the vegetation of the marsh. It was partially frozen, which meant you could walk on the ice and suddenly hit a muskrat trail or a warm spot and fall through ice into the deep mud and cold water of the swamp. For the few that relish it, this environment creates great pheasant hunting, but it's not without its perils. Cent had charged hard into the cattails and, now in his seventh year, he was as good as he would ever get. Most dogs peak at about that age. They're physically at their best or slightly on a decline and they are perfectly experienced. Even though he was lighter and had better weight distribution than me, he too would occasionally break through the ice. He was rousting pheasants, which had secreted themselves into this 30-acre marsh and were now exploding from the cover.

I never saw the encounter begin and I never saw it end; I couldn't get there. At some point that afternoon, things changed from a fun hunt to a life-and-death struggle. Cent had fought and encountered coons all his life in North America. He had dispatched dozens of them. Sometimes he would handle them two or even three at a time. More often he and Jäger and Gretchen would take them on as a team and would make short order of them, each dog knowing his or her role, job and function. Raccoons have made their way north over the last 50 years; encounters have gone from rare to occasional to frequent to ubiquitous, as they live in cities, suburbs and the country.

Today as the barking and growling began, I suspected it was a coon; then I heard the hissing and knew it for a fact. I tried to make my way toward the fight, but broke through the ice and couldn't get back up on top. This limited my mobility as I broke ice and busted through mud and cattails with each step.

The howls, screams, scratching and biting and the splashing and suffering of both Cent and the coon were very audible to me, but I could see nothing in the thick swamp. I continued to use the stock of my gun to break ice, but the process was slow and my progress minimal. I could hear now that something was being pushed under the water; it could have been Cent or the coon, I couldn't tell. Then I heard his woof, woof, woof and I knew it was Cent, and he was now free. I could hear them re-engage with the snarling, hissing, barking, nipping. I knew that Cent's best move was to get behind the coon, grab it by the back of its neck and snap the body with one move, breaking its back. Without firm ground this action doesn't work; he couldn't create the torque in the water. This match would end in bites, drowning or escape.

I knew Cent will not back down. He usually had allies, but Jäger was still in rehabilitation and Gretchen was delivering puppies and I was struggling with ice, mud and cold.

The skirmish rekindled and became as ferocious as any I'd ever heard. Evidently they both had renewed vigor; I could hear them back on the ice. My hopes soared as I knew this was Cent's best chance for his back-break. Suddenly I could hear the ice break and the splash as one fell into the icy water. From the sounds I could tell it was Cent. Then I heard a thump. Rather than escape, the racoon jumped onto Cent's back to try to drown him. They were now within 20 yards, but that's a long way in a frozen thick swamp. Suddenly it was quiet. I could hear low pitched "grrrs" and thrashing, but none of the violent sounds. I broke ice even faster, fearing Cent was underwater. As I broke into a small clearing, I saw the victorious Cent Von Esterfeld holding in his mouth a 50-pound-plus raccoon, very recently drowned in a violent struggle. It was he who had twisted the coon into the water and kept him down until dead. In the process the coon had bitten Cent's legs and ears severely; his nose was also deeply scratched and there were numerous bites and puncture wounds in his mouth and on his head. Now that the assault was over, he was once again his dignified self as he presented to me his quarry, the largest coon I've ever seen. I was angry, relieved, wet, cold, tired and so happy that I hadn't lost Cent that afternoon.

A week later, Cent and I were hunting in South Dakota. He had enjoyed a good morning and we were finding birds quite easily. I had taken a break for lunch and was now ready to get back in the field. As I grabbed my gun, I looked to see my old friend Cent get up and then collapse. I rushed to him. He couldn't get back up.

I was shaken and concerned to the point that I left the field to find a vet. Could there have been a snake? I thought. Did he have a heart attack, a stroke? I couldn't imagine what had just happened to the strongest dog I've ever owned. The vet opened his shop and a half hour later said, "I haven't the slightest idea what's wrong, but he appears to be paralyzed from the neck down. I'm sorry, but I have no idea why."

The call to Kath was horrible. She loved Cent and I knew so little, I didn't know what to tell her. It was a day later that we got the news: Cent Von Esterfeld had contracted a disease called Coonhound Paralysis. It was a result of the previous week's fight to the death; not a lot is known about the disease except it seems to come from an exchange of saliva between the coon and the dog. The effects take place one week later when the infected dog becomes paralyzed from the neck down, and every dog that has ever had it has died. The prognosis couldn't have been worse. Kath couldn't accept it and I was crushed.

She researched the University of Iowa, which seemed to be the only place that had studied the problem at all and discovered that the reason all the dogs die from it is because their owners put them down after the diagnosis. This simple fact, combined with her own stubbornness, created the first Coonhound Paralysis Ward in history, right in the bedroom of our house. She brought up a blue children's swimming pool, we filled it with straw and laid the paralyzed Cent into the pool. We fed him a ground mixture of venison burger and rice, but he had very little appetite. While alert, he was truly paralyzed, and he was further traumatized that he had to pee on himself and crap in the pool.

His body began to atrophy and the weight slipped off him; he went from 82 pounds down to 70, then to 60, then even lower.

Jäger would visit him as tenderly as a spouse visits her mate in a nursing home. She would lick his head and lie down with him in the pool. You could see him relax and read the appreciation in his eyes. The straw would get changed, the food ground, the mess cleaned up and still no improvement, no help or advice from the vets, no probable outcome except death — now a slow, erosive death.

Then Kath started doing physical therapy with the dog; we would move his legs to try to maintain muscle tone and give him some exercise. Whether it worked or not, it made everybody feel better.

Two months had gone by. I had come home to change from a business suit into hunting clothes to head off to the club for a hunt. The mentally alert Cent recognized my change of clothes. As I emerged from the toilet, standing there in the straw in a little kid's blue swimming pool was a gaunt and weak Cent Von Esterfeld. It was the first time he had stood in the two months since that morning in South Dakota. I rushed to him and yelled, "Kath! Kath!" He collapsed, but he was moving his legs, trying to get up again, something he couldn't have done that morning.

She stepped in the room, saw the movement and said, "By God, we may have won this fight."

As I left the room and went down the back stairs of our house, the stairs the dogs always used, I reached the kitchen and heard a huge tumbling sound on the stairs. It was the sound of a fragile, but willing, German Shorthair who had struggled out of the pool, made it to the stairs — and had then fallen all the way down! There he lay as I rushed to him. His eyes said, "Don't leave me, I want to go with you."

We checked him over, and nothing was broken. He never spent one more day in that little kid's blue swimming pool. He was now back on a dog bed, doing therapy and, within weeks, running with me in the mornings. He was the first dog known to survive Coonhound Paralysis, and he did it because we wouldn't give up on him and he never gave up on us. From that day on he would be known as Mr. Cent, a noble title he had earned.

DOING WHAT
WE ALL LOVE MOST

When I grew up in south Minneapolis, back in the days of Rex and Duke, there were three brothers, all in my grade in school. Greg, Jeff and George Bruestle were a set of twins and a younger brother, all in the same class. Each had their own set of friends, and their mother, Mabel, became a "den mother" for us all. At their house, many lifelong friendships were formed.

In the seventies, George would go off to Alaska to build the pipeline; as an electrician he prospered and made enough money to have a grub stake with which to start his own business. We became roommates when he returned, and his son, Jason, spent a lot of time with us from the time he was eight to 12 years old. Jason wanted to be a hunter for as long as I'd known him.

Jason had hunted with me since he was 12 years old, and 15 years later, he was no longer a boy to teach — he was a man to hunt with. While I've always loved bird hunting first and everything else second, he loves big game first and birds second.

After the two of us had driven 16 hours across the prairie — racking up one speeding ticket, and another warning — we were close to our destination in northwestern North Dakota. In the back of the Suburban were three German shorthairs. Without them we wouldn't have taken this December trip. Without them we wouldn't have taken two trips in November, three in October and two in September. Without them we wouldn't have walked six to eight hours a day through cornfields, forest, sloughs and sand hills. Without them we wouldn't have known the endorphin rush our bodies could deliver or the profound silence two men experience when they let three dogs lead the way.

On this trip, our quarry would be pheasants, for sure, sharptail maybe, Huns possibly. Scott Pearson, a nice guy, good hunter and aspiring outfitter, had invited us and met us there. His father had been one of my football coaches in college and we were there to check out the territory. After a quick snack and introductions, with three hours till dark, we hit the field and within minutes three German shorthairs were locked on point. We were impressed, but the point looked "soft" to my experienced eye. As Jason and Scott moved into position, it suddenly became clear why. The point suddenly broke into a scuffle and the quiet was shattered, not with the burr of wings but with the snarling and barking of dogs.

I yelled "coonfight!" and rushed to the scene. My heart sank as I approached the combatants to see all three tearing away and sparring not with a coon, but with a North Dakota porcupine. Despite the fact that there were hundreds of quills embedded in the dogs' muzzles, mouths, ears and paws, they were getting the best of the porcupine — at least for now. After any great prize fight, there is always a period of days when the winner wonders if he really won, as he deals with the aches, pains and injuries of the confrontation. After 16 hours on the road, $150 in speeding tickets and $170 in licensing costs, it took just 15 minutes of hunting to determine that we wouldn't harvest only birds.

As we left the field, the wounded warriors would strike point, a bird would rise, we'd shoot and Gretchen, the most reliable dog I've ever owned, ran over and, despite dozens and dozens of quills in her tongue, gums and mouth, would retrieve the bird to hand. It pained me to see how tough she really was. We spent the next two hours in a farmhouse basement, cutting and pulling hundreds of quills out of three "victorious" shorthairs.

We dealt with the dogs one at a time. Until you really have to deal with this kind of mess, you don't know how difficult it is for everyone. You need a good light, a pair of scissors, needle-nose pliers, lots of clean rags and a big stick. The process includes cutting the quills with scissors to let the pressure out, pulling the quills out with the pliers, cleaning up the blood with the rags. You use the stick to hold the dog's mouth open as you pull the quills from out of the gums, tongue, throat and roof of the mouth. You never really understand the meaning of the word *stoicism* until you deal with a "porcupined" dog. They seem to intuitively know that, even though this is all very painful, you are actually trying to help them. Despite your best efforts, you never really get all the quills out and some break off in the process. Inevitably you end up at the vet, but this effort will at least get you back in the field for a couple of days.

The next day we would start early, which you can do in North Dakota. The hunting was excellent. In those days, the limits were four per day, per person and we would have our 12 birds by 1:00 p.m. and then shift over to sharptail, which we'd hunt till dark. The dogs would hunt full bore from sunrise to sunset, they'd be cold in the morning, wet several times throughout the day, hot in the afternoon and tired at night. I don't know if hunters ever feel closer to their dogs than after a long day afield. You know that you're tired, thirsty, hungry and wet. You've walked 12 to 15 miles through all kinds of variable terrain and cover. You also know that your dogs have run at least three times as far as you have and are as tired, thirsty and hungry as you are, and that they were in cover even tougher than where you walked.

On the North Dakota prairie where the towns are few and far between, Jason and I were headed to the nearest town some 35 miles from where we stopped hunting for the day. Scott headed home. The Suburban was full of the smells that mark the end of a long day — two sweaty, wet hunters, three wet dogs, and 18 pheasants and sharptail. To non-hunters, the smell might be offensive, but to a hunter, it smelled like success. We pulled into town and our destination was the only motel. As we entered the lobby, we saw a sign that read: "No Dogs." Then another: "Absolutely No Dogs." And yet another: "Don't Even Ask About Bringing Your Dog in the Room!"

My rule is we're a team and we all stay together at the end of the day. I never leave a dog alone in the room, I offer to leave a deposit in case of damage, I'll even offer to pay more, but my dogs stay with me — that's it. The owner of the motel came to the desk and we exchanged pleasantries. We asked for one large room, and as if we never saw a sign, I explained that we had three dogs.

He responded like a lightning bolt, "Well, they aren't coming in here."

My temper began to rise, but with firm self-control I explained, "They're housedogs that hunt and I'd be glad to pay more or offer a deposit if you'd prefer."

"No dogs," he snapped back.

I explained like a trained salesman that "these dogs have stayed in hotels all over the country, without any incident" and that I would be glad to guarantee that.

"No dogs — period," he said.

I then pointed out that it was late, that his motel seemed very empty and that without the dogs we were leaving. "Fine," he said, "the next motel is 50 miles that way," he pointed north, "50 miles that way," he pointed west or "50 miles that way," he pointed south.

Hopefully, I asked "What about east?"

"100 miles," he sneered.

"Jason, we're headed west," I said as we walked out. "And you, sir, can head directly to hell."

Back in the truck we faced the reality of a 50-mile drive, but felt good about standing up for "the team." Now, Jason is good at many things, but one of the things he's best at is sleeping, and it doesn't matter if he's cold, wet, tired and hungry, this boy can sleep. That night he demonstrated his abilities and so did three shorthairs in the back. My father always taught me an empty stomach produces more gas than a full one, and that night, as I quietly drove, the snores echoed from all four and the farts wafted through the truck with alarming regularity, and they acted like smelling salts to keep me awake.

Suddenly, in the distance I could see the lights of our destination in the night sky. As my spirits lifted, I felt the truck pulling strongly to the right, and the sound of a vehicle clipping down the road transitioned to a thumping sound from the right rear. The sound was loud enough to even wake Jason.

We scrambled to unpack the full Suburban to get out a spare tire and other necessary equipment. Out came the guns, birds, dogs, dog kennels and packs. It was after 8:00 p.m., dark, getting colder and, as if on cue, started to snow. We got the tire changed, repacked all the gear and limped into town on our spare tire, which like many, was low on air. We pulled up to the only motel in town and walked in. A smiling lady who owned the place welcomed us. "We've driven a long way," I said, "and we have three dogs."

"I love dogs," she said, and we all relaxed.

The restaurant in town was open and they served big steaks and great hash browns. The team slept well that night in room number 18, with three dogs in a ball, one head resting on the butt of the next. Before we fell asleep, we all wrassled on the floor of the room to show each other how happy we were to be together. Two tired hunters and three tired dogs, playing like boys and puppies, celebrating the end of a long day of camaraderie, doing what we all love most.

THE END TO A HUNT

They were both young, smart, good-looking and successful. One knew how to hunt and was good at it. The other was new to the field and this was just a day out of the office for him. John Allen would become one of the Twin Cities' top real-estate brokers and investors. By 45 he would be rich and retire to Florida. Glib, and with the looks of a movie star, he was a guest at the club that day for a pheasant and turkey hunt. Eric Bischoff was a martial-arts expert who was dabbling in pro-wresting as a ring announcer. He eventually excelled as a wrestler, first with Ted Turner and then with Vince McMahon, and he played a key role in the sport as it got more and more complicated. He also produced films and wrote books, but on this day he was working at the club as a hunting guide, using his top tournament dog, Hombre, as a guide dog. John and Eric had never met before that day.

Hombre found six pheasants, pointed them all, and as John Allen and his party shot them, Hombre would retrieve them to Eric's hand. Even the inexperienced eye could see Hombre was special and a real talented hunting dog. He found three more pheasants and two of the three were shot, with only one getting away. Then he struck an odd point. It lacked the intensity of most points; the tail flagged. It's the kind of point good dogs throw when they're onto a skunk, coon or possum. In this case it was a wild turkey. The turkey broke and ran with Hombre on its tail. There was confusion in the tall cover. The turkey chose not to fly, but continued to run. Suddenly a shotgun roared and the turkey kept running, but Hombre didn't.

"My God, my God!" Eric yelled as he fell to his knees and embraced his tournament hunting partner. The dog's eyes were rolled back; there was no sign of breathing. In seconds the fun autumn afternoon had descended into cries of grief. While Hombre had felt little pain, Eric was feeling a lot of it, knowing he had just lost his five-year-old male German shorthair pointer. John and the others crowded around, searching for words that didn't come. Finally John said, "I did it. I did it. It was me."

Eric kept holding Hombre and couldn't speak. Then John said, "I'll make it good." Everyone knew he had a big checkbook and was as honest as the day is long. The hunt was over, the good memories fogged by the tragedy. No one would brag about their shooting over beers; they would only recollect the one "boom," that single shot at a running turkey that would have been best let go.

I was at the club that afternoon; John told me what had

happened and repeated that he'd pay for the dog, but asked that I be the intermediary. I agreed to do so. I rushed to Eric who was still in the field. He was, at the time, one of my most formidable competitors in tournament hunting. He would run hard and often against my teammates and me, trying to best us in the field, every tournament, every time. He was a strong, talented hunter and Hombre was his best dog. I sat down next to him and looked at the dead athlete that had beaten me often. We both had tears in our eyes. We didn't talk. If it were Jäger or Cent, I don't know that I could have felt any worse. Seeing a great talent wasted is a sad thing. Quietly we removed Hombre's body. Later I told Eric about John's intentions. He said he'd think about it and call me.

Two days later Eric called. He said he thought that the price should be $7,000. The minute I heard the number, I thought it was high, but I was afraid that if I said so, I'd be out of line or, worse yet, demeaning a great dog. Cent had cost me $5,000, excellent pups were $1,000 at the time and it cost about $2,000 to train them to completion. Hombre had thousands of dollars in birds on him, had won several thousand dollars in prize money the previous year in tournaments and he was central to Eric's family and existence. I agreed to float the number, but I didn't look forward to the call. John responded as I expected. He wasn't a dog owner, he wasn't really a hunter and what started as a casual afternoon with the boys had now become a complete pain in his ass.

After some chitchat, I told him "Eric is thinking $7,000." There was stunned silence on the other end.

"Bill, I wasn't thinking anything like that!" John said.

Knowing I had a problem, I asked, "What were you thinking, John?"

"Oh, a grand or two, but not seven," he said.

We talked a little and I explained puppy prices, training costs, bird costs, tournament checks — all the things that went into Eric's number, sometimes feeling my comments were fair, sometimes feeling like I was pushing it. John was never obstinate or cheap; he was a little naïve, but he was not reneging from his promise to make it right. Then as we talked, it struck me he could never, ever grasp the intangibles of this situation. He could never understand the value of knowing your dog is waiting for you. The warmth of sitting on the floor with the dog on your lap or rolling around playing and wrasslin' like you were 12 years old again. He didn't know how hard it was to feel 12 years old again for any amount of money. He didn't realize that the dog was Eric's personal trainer. John wouldn't know that after long days afield, Eric would lie on the floor and fall asleep with Hombre curled up next to him. He didn't know the value of a guard dog that saved you from worrying about your wife and family when you weren't home. Finally, John offered $3,000. He felt stretched, but wanted to get it over with.

When I told Eric about John's offer, he was angry and let down. "I thought he was a man of his word," was his instant response.

I let him vent. Then I said, "He's approaching this like a business deal, like a real-estate transaction or an insurance settlement — very rational, very cool. He's not a dog guy, but ultimately he seems to think everything has a price and $7,000 is just too high."

Over the next 15 minutes Eric repeated why it wasn't too high. I understood both points of view. We agreed to talk the next day. Eric said he'd accept $5,000. He said, "I don't like it, but I'll do it."

I agreed to talk to John. We talked and then he said it, the words I wouldn't forget and have heard in various ways at other times in my life since then — the words that separate dog people from non-dog people. "Okay, Bill, I'll go $4,000 to get it over with or else it goes to my insurance people and they'll never pay that much. After all, it is just a dog."

I respected his offer, his approach, his detachment. I didn't resent his statement; I just knew that it was the primary difference between him and me. I've never said it, never thought it, and I've never acted like there is such a thing as "just a dog."

DOGS JUST AREN'T
FOR FISHIN'

Even the best dogs are generally a pain when you're fishing. Dogs just aren't for fishing. As much as I loved Cent, who by age eight was "Mr. Cent," he was always a loser when it came to fishing. I remember the day I snuck out to go fishing. Cent never noticed as I quietly motored away from the dock, hoping not to wake him. I was fishing 500 yards away when he amazingly saw me, jumped in the lake and swam to me "woofing" all the way. When he got to me, he proceeded to swim in circles around the boat "woofing" as loudly as he could for 15 minutes, tangling my fish line, eating one bobber and scaring every fish in the area away.

I had one old friend who always took his dog fishing. The golden retriever would sit up in the bow of the boat, looking beautiful and important at the same time. The dog never jumped in the lake, never ate bobbers, never got hooked and never woofed. One day my friend went to the bow, where the dog always sat. He grabbed his anchor to throw it overboard and secure his fishing spot. As the anchor flew and the rope unraveled, the retriever had unwittingly caught its foot in the rope and flew out of the boat tied to the anchor and destined for a drowning. My friend, in an act of Popeye-like heroism, grabbed a knife, jumped overboard and swam down the rope. He cut the dog loose, he cut the dog and he cut himself. Everybody lived, except the anchor. Dogs just aren't for fishing.

One weekend I went fishing out at Long Tom Farm, one of my favorite prairie places where the lake is full of fish of all types and sizes. I was casting from shore with a slip bobber and worm, just like kids do. It made me feel young and as I was two days away from a birthday, that was just how this boomer wanted to feel. I was with Fritz and Mixx, both grandsons of Mr. Cent; Fritz was a multiple champion and Mixx was willing and obedient. On my first cast both dogs jumped in the lake and then fought over who would retrieve my bobber. Fritz got hooked in the process and Mixx was completely tangled in the line. Dogs just aren't for fishing.

After catching several small bass, I got a real bite. Big, strong and powerful, this fish was controlling me instead of me controlling it. With ultra-light equipment and four-pound test, I was clearly outclassed. The only advantage I had was the bank was steep, and so I could gain height on the fish and let him run, and I could run sideways on the bank to tire him out. To the fish's advantage were ten yards of cat-tails between me and the open water, several stumps, my insufficient equipment and the fact I had no net. To a handicapper, the fish was a sure bet to win.

After 15 minutes of fight, the fish was tired and I made my move. I slowly came down to the shore, picked a spot where the cattails were a little thinner and tried to bring the big one in. It moved well at first and then I could feel its big belly dragging on weeds and mud; it would go no further easily. At this point about six yards out lay an 11-pound carp, the top third exposed, held by a four-pound line and number-three hook. Out of ideas I said, "Fetch 'em up" and two German shorthairs sprang into the water, grabbed the fish at the same time and retrieved it together, right to hand. With soft mouths they didn't leave a scar. I was now holding one of the ugliest and certainly most surprised fish in history. The duo would repeat the feat 20 minutes later on a 12-pounder. It was the first time I ever thought, dogs just might be for fishing.

THE EXTENDED LINE . . .

While most of The Line is genetically linked, there have been exceptions like Merry Maker, Halley and — much later — Chevy, who were brought into the group as outcrosses to freshen The Line or introduce desired characteristics. In the "Extended Line" there are the dogs we care about that live in other people's houses; they're not all hunting dogs either. My sister Bonnie, who figured out Duke's name so long ago now, lives in California, and her first dog, Paddie, actually came as chattel when she bought her house there. This half-golden retriever and half-shepherd was a 100-pound bruiser who loved my sister and brother-in-law, hated mail carriers and was very racist, barking ferociously at all black people, friend or stranger. When my sister and brother-in-law bought their house in the mid-eighties, Bonnie was a TV actress and Gerry an agent in Hollywood. The seller thought Paddie would be miserable if he had to leave the house so he would only sell his San Fernando Valley home to a buyer who would also take the dog. My sister liked the dog better than the house. While I'm quite sure the bank saw it as a typical real-estate mortgage, I think it was more a dog finance plan. They all got on famously and, as part of the deal, they didn't sell the house until Paddie passed on, so that he'd never have to move out of it.

When it came time to replace Paddie, who we considered part of the "Extended Line," I thought a golden retriever would be perfect and offered to help find one. I had started a search when the phone rang from L.A. It was Bonnie.

"Billy?"

"Yeah. How you doin'?" I asked.

"Great! I've got big news!"

"What's up? What's the secret?"

"We've got a dog!" she exclaimed.

"Wow, what have you got?" I asked.

"It's from the pound and it's a cross, part shepherd, part husky, with blue eyes. It's sooo cute," she gushed.

I almost dropped the phone. A pound dog! A cross, part shepherd and part husky with blue eyes! This was the worst idea I'd ever heard. I believe blue-eyed huskies are wolf crosses and I don't trust them. While shepherds can be the smartest of dogs, husky crosses aren't usually very bright and they can be very hard to train. But did I say that? No, I said, "Wow, that's great. I can't wait to see it!" I didn't mean a word.

At five months, the new dog, Buster, was sent off to training, and just as he entered the Extended Line, Bonnie became pregnant with her first baby. They had just bought a new house, had a baby on the way and now owned an untrained, hyperactive, blue-eyed dog with a wolf gene that was already driving them nuts. This was no Paddie; he was a slow learner, disobedient, chewed on everything and was starting to bare his teeth in response to orders he didn't like. As she told me about the training plan, I began to realize that I was a dog snob. While I had spent my entire youth and numerous years of my adult life longing for a dog, any dog, of any breed or mix, I had become an elitist. It didn't feel good. I listened to the training plan, checked my biases and reached back to my younger self who worked as hard to return a mongrel as a registered Great Dane.

"This guy is a famous trainer in the Hollywood Hills. He's on TV all the time, has a big, nice kennel. I think he'll do a great job," she said.

I thought to myself, "All this for a mutt?" but I didn't say it out loud. The closest I came was to say, "Are you sure about putting money into that dog?"

"Oh yeah, Billy, he'll be fine."

Admittedly, her career was doing very well. She had a sitcom on NBC — she was costarring in *We Got it Made* and was making big bucks. But the wolf gene concerned me.

"Would you come out and check on the training progress in a few weeks?" she asked.

"Of course I'll be there. I'll be glad to," I said. I began to get weekly reports on the dog's progress, or lack thereof. The "trainer to the stars" was getting $500 per week in 1985. That was big money, but it was her money. What concerned me was that there seemed to be no progress in obedience and the growling hadn't stopped. Before I went out to see Buster in person, I said to Bonnie, "You know I love dogs and this Buster might work out, but if he's not coming around I think I should shoot it for you and just get it over with. How do you feel about that?"

"Oh, you'll see. He'll be fine, don't worry. You don't need to shoot anything."

It sounds horrible, but sometimes the most important thing you can do with a dog is recognize if it's a menace. Few people will make that tough call until it's too late; either someone has been hurt or an innocent dog has been injured. I had a bad feeling about Buster and I brought my gun along in case.

I went to see the Hollywood dog trainer and met Buster for the first time. His eyes were indeed blue, a light blue, and he noticeably sized people up. He was very aggressive in his kennel and his bark was harsh and intimidating. At about 65 pounds and still growing, he looked more like a husky than a shepherd. I didn't see any shepherd characteristics, and the more I looked at him, the more I thought he was a wolf-husky cross and not shepherd at all.

When I met the trainer I was very blunt with him. He knew I was in the business and I asked his honest assessment of the dog. He gave me the old blah, blah, blah that you tell people to keep their dog in training. Finally I asked him, "Do you see anything that this dog is really good at?"

He hesitated and said, "No."

"Has he been aggressive with you?"

He hesitated and said, "Yes."

"If he were your dog, would you put any time, money or effort into him?"

He looked at the ground and said, "If that were the standard, every dog trainer in America would be out of business." He was right, my question was unfair.

Together we approached Buster, whom he had been training for six weeks. He couldn't handle on leash, couldn't handle well to voice commands and didn't demonstrate basic obedience. Buster looked hopeless to me.

Then the trainer said, "I know what you're doing with your line of shorthairs, and that's great. It makes training fast, easy and cheap, and you get great dogs. But you have to understand most people will scrimp on the front side, buy dogs cheap or take free dogs and then pay big money to train them, feed them and vet them for the rest of their lives. Most people wouldn't recognize a well-bred dog in the first place and don't understand its value. Your sister wants a pet; I'll give her a pet."

We shook hands and agreed to meet in six weeks. I had to agree conceptually with what he said. To me, Buster was a waste of time and money, but Buster wasn't my dog. We talked on the phone almost weekly and there seemed to be little or no progress. One day I said, "Bon, I don't think there's really any shepherd there, so there's not much to work with. Do you understand?" She said she did, but I'm not sure if she did. Most people wouldn't. With selection and care, good breeders reinforce desirable traits and qualities. Most breeders don't want extremely aggressive behavior so they breed it out. They do want sociability, so they breed it in. If, for example, pit bulls are bred to fight, they are bred for the fight over and over again. This will usually result in increasingly aggressive fighters. If pit bulls are bred to be family dogs, you breed away from the fight and they become very domestic. In only five years of thoughtful breeding, entire lines of a breed can have totally different traits and qualities. Five years can represent five to eight generations. Dog generations move very quickly, so changes and adjustments happen fast. Chances are you have no idea of your own family history five to eight generations back. In my case, five generations go back to the mid-1700s and eight generations to the 16th century.

For centuries, wolves were not successfully domesticated. As a matter of fact, many will argue that they're not domesticated now, though there have been domestic breeding programs for decades. I would argue that's not long enough. Shepherds have 50,000 years of selection in their history, under a lot of significant human influence. This is not inconsequential.

When I went back to L.A., Buster was slightly better behaved, but he could still only be handled by the trainer-to-the-stars himself. He wouldn't work for my sister, my brother-in-law, me or even the trainer's assistants. The dog was a loser in my mind and I coldly offered to shoot it. My offer was declined and he was booked for four more weeks, which brought the training bill up to $5,000 (about twice that much in today's dollars).

They brought the dog home at the end of six more weeks with a total bill of $5,500. He was still aggressive, had only basic obedience and needed to be re-housebroken, but everybody was happy. I was basically told to mind my own business and not to bring any guns around when I visited. Bonnie was only weeks from delivering when she dropped a towel on the floor. As she reached over to pick it up, Buster bared his teeth and growled deeply. He had taken a liking to the towel. Bonnie backed off. The trust was broken.

Due to the impending arrival, a different mentality set in. Kids' toys have a way of drifting into houses even before the baby arrives. Shortly after the towel incident, Buster took ownership of a toy building block. As Bonnie reached to pick it up he snarled and bared his teeth. I got the call. She explained what had happened. I said I'd come out next week on business and take care of the problem, and in the meantime, why not put the dog back with the trainer. My solution would be quick and final.

As I prepared for my trip, Bonnie called and told me, "We've given Buster to the Shapons. They just love him and want him, so we delivered him this morning." The Shapons were two guys, a gay couple, who were good friends of Bonnie and Gerry.

"What are you doing?" I asked loudly. "That dog is dangerous and shouldn't be with people."

"Oh, Billy, they don't have kids, they're both men and they love Buster. They always have," she responded. The issue was closed.

Six months later, Buster viciously attacked one of the Shapons, tearing his left arm to shreds. It took over 200 stitches to put him back together and the injury led to permanent disability. They, too, refused my offer to deal with the dog. Buster attacked twice more before he was finally put down.

As much as I love dogs and admire people who love and care for them, there are certain dogs that should be selected out of the gene pool; in other words, terminated. It is crushing to be forced to make this decision. I've never offered to shoot a dog without feeling sadness and even misgivings, but I know in the long run that it's the right thing to do, so I make the offer.

THE HEROLDS

I hunted northeast Iowa for over 15 years and had harvested numerous pheasants in the area. One of the farms I visited regularly belonged to Jack Herold. He and his wife, Ann, are a fine couple who have raised a good family; they grew corn and beans a good part of their lives on about 400 acres of prime Iowa farmland. The soil there is black and the yields are excellent. They also planted trees, picked berries, made wine and preserves and shucked black walnuts — they shared it all. I rarely went to see them without bringing a present because they were always so generous with me. The biggest gift they gave everyone was their trees.

Iowa farmland is expensive and productive. Most farmers drain and tile whatever of it they can and cut or bulldoze the trees and groves to have more land to farm. Jack and Ann would plant groves of trees and cover for wildlife of all kinds. It would, in turn, attract deer, pheasant, squirrels, rabbits, wild turkeys and game species, but also songbirds and many non-game species. They would even plant walnut trees, which can take a generation to grow to any useful size. While most people plant things for their own benefit — flowers, gardens, row crops, landscaping or forestry trees — they planted trees for others to enjoy even after they would be gone. Jack and Ann went on Peace Corps missions to help people in other parts of the world with agriculture.

Next door on a farm of similar size, about a half mile away, lived Jack's cousin Cletus Herold. Cletus and Anita had raised three boys and a girl; two of those boys, Tim and Matt, became very important to The Line. They became my good friends and teammates. For years I didn't need to knock on their door for permission to hunt their land when visiting Jack. Things change as they do in the country, and one November day I found myself knocking on the door of a new home just built there.

Without realizing it, I was approaching the house Matt had moved into. I was soon met by a growling, snarling 85-pound Weimaraner on a chain. Weimaraners can be marvelous field dogs and they certainly can be good-looking, but they have a tendency to be "one-man dogs" and quite protective. This certainly seemed to be the case with Rusty. With all the barking and snapping and growling, Matt came out and asked me what was going on.

"I was coming up to ask permission to hunt and the dog attacked me," I told him. "He not only growled and barked, he snapped with intent to harm; only the chain saved me from a severe bite." Matt immediately reprimanded the dog with appropriate discipline. (It's always hard to discipline a dog after an incident rather than in the moment.) He told me to go ahead and hunt, which I did. When I was done, I dropped back to the house to thank him. At the door the Weimaraner was back to his aggressive behavior. Matt asked me what I thought.

Hesitantly I told him, "What I've seen here, in my opinion, is likely to continue and probably get worse." I could see Rusty was about two years old; he was a beautiful, big, strong dog.

"Is he aggressive with other dogs, too, or just people?" I asked.

"I don't know," Matt said. "He seems to hunt fine with other dogs."

"Well, my guess is that you're going to have more trouble with his protectiveness. I just hope it's not some neighbor kid. Do you have children?"

"No, we don't, but we might some day. What would you do?"

I hesitated, but finally I said coldly, "I'd keep my eyes open and if it becomes a pattern, I'd get rid of the dog."

I've had to choke dogs, hit dogs, jolt dogs and flip dogs to get them to come around. Flipping dogs entails catching a dog during unwanted violent behavior and physically wrestling it onto its back and choking it into submission. If you watch wolves, you see that the alpha wolf does more or less this same thing to force others in the pack to submit. Only by placing a dog on its back and then applying as much pressure as appropriate can one submit an aggressive dog. If this technique doesn't work, you'll be in over your head and the dog may need to be dispatched. Wrestling a strong, aggressive 70- or 85-pound dog into submission is not easy and once you start "flipping," you had better succeed before you quit.

It was four weeks later and I got a phone call from Matt. "How ya doin'?" He asked, sounding upbeat.

"Good, good. How about you?" I responded. I was surprised to hear from him, but I was pleased that he'd called.

"I've got a problem," he said. "That damn Rusty has done exactly what you said he'd do. He's attacked several people and I have to do something."

"I'm sorry, that's too bad. I hoped it wouldn't happen this way."

"Well, it has and that's why I'm calling. I don't have the heart to do it myself and I was wondering if you'd shoot him for me?"

Now, shooting dogs is one crappy job and I just hate it, but I couldn't blame him for not wanting to do it himself. I couldn't shoot one of my own either, but it's expensive to use a vet and there's a kind of *Old Yeller* outdoorsman tradition of taking care of things yourself that holds over to the modern day. I hesitated and then said "yes," but I explained that I wouldn't be down in Iowa for several months, hoping that would get me off the hook.

"Oh, this can't wait for several months," he said, "I'll have to come up there."

"Well, you're more than welcome. When do you want to come?"

We arranged for Matt and his brother Tim — who became two of my best friends and teammates — to visit me, get a tour of the club and leave me a big, mean Weimaraner to shoot. The world can be so strange sometimes.

It was March and I got to thinking about Matt's problem. I knew if it were me, I wouldn't want to be without a dog, so I checked out the kennel and found that I had a hardworking, pro hunting dog named Jiggs that I could afford to give away on a sad occasion like this one. So I got Matt's surprise ready. When they arrived with their wives I got my first look at Tim Herold, Matt's older brother, who would eventually become one of the best tournament hunters in history. He was six-foot five-inches tall, strong and powerful. A former college football player, he was now known as the "Concrete Man," as he was in the cement business. I then sprang the Jiggs idea on the group and they wanted to meet him. Off they went hunting with Jiggs, and when they came back they said, "Thanks, that would be really great!" From that day forward, the Herold brothers would never be without one or several dogs from The Line.

I had taken Rusty and put him in the kennel for me to deal with later. After saying goodbye to the Herold boys, their wives and Jiggs, I knew I couldn't put if off any longer. I grabbed my pistol, a .357 Magnum and went to the holding kennel to terminate Rusty. I didn't relish dropping this brute, but the situation didn't allow for any other outcome. When I looked in the kennel, Rusty was gone! I searched up and down the 20 kennels inside and out, but no Rusty. I began to ask anyone around. Then the kennel boy spoke up.

"Chalupsky took him," he stammered.

"What?"

"Chalupsky took him. I saw him drive away." Mike Chalupsky was our dog trainer and he was an important part of building The Line in its early years.

"Why that son of a bitch!" I said out loud.

I had told him about my agreement with the Herolds. The old softy couldn't stand me shooting that snarly Rusty, so he had stolen him! I tried to call him all weekend, but he never answered. When I finally reached him, he denied having the dog. Finally I said, "A guy could get fired for stealing, you know?"

"I suppose he could, but only if he stole something of value," he said. "A dead dog ain't worth much, is it?"

Mike hid Rusty in his six-dog menagerie in an isolated place in the country for over five years.

"I use him as a clean-up dog, Bill," he told me. "When all the other dogs are tired and cold, I get him out to find the last birds. He doesn't hurt me or the other dogs and nobody else comes around."

Mike became more and more confident in Rusty and began to trust him in different situations. One night at a field trial, Rusty got loose and tore up three other dogs and terrorized men, women and children for over 15 minutes before Mike could catch him. Even then Mike continued to hide him until one day he was training dogs and Rusty and another dog collided at full speed. (Dogs do just run into each other sometimes in their frenzy.) Rusty died two days later from the impact.

WILLY

One of the most important aspects of building The Line has been the role of teammates. We use their homes to keep, nurture and develop talent. In reality, the most dogs that we can keep at our house at one time is about five; at the kennels at the club we can keep up to 30, but they should be working/breeding dogs under four years old, if possible. While we could certainly keep older dogs at the kennel, we prefer not to. We try to place dogs into good homes by their fourth or fifth year; our perspective is they deserve it. Some of these dogs have ended up in great homes with super people and loving families. These dogs — like Sadie, Cruzer, Max and Heidi, who we placed with friends, relatives and club members — led privileged lives.

If one is coldly calculating, most dogs live about 12 years; the first two years are developmental. Years three to seven are highly productive in terms of breeding, competition and potential field success. The years eight to 12 are progressively slower and less productive. For the family with one dog, you can assume then that you have about five highly productive years out of every twelve. If you stagger your dogs by ages, you can increase their number of productive years — with two dogs five years apart in age, you should have ten productive years out of fifteen and so on. By placing dogs with great potential into teammates' homes (keeping generally the rights for competition and breeding), we can have top performing dogs on a constant basis. The Line on any given day may have dogs with Bruce and Lori Wohlrabe, Matt and Lori Herold, Tim Herold and Paula, Andy and Shelly Miller, Bob Burditt and Kristi Johnson, plus what we might keep ourselves. All of these people are members of our U.S. Team, friends or employees who really care about dogs and talent. These dogs will usually live their lives in great homes and they, too, have privileged lives and great launching pads for competition and breeding. Without this practice, The Line would be limited to the confines of one house and a kennel with the constant reality that old dogs take up large amounts of space.

I've also believed for decades now that the old axiom that "real hunting dogs shouldn't be in the house, they should be in the kennel" is pure hogwash. There have been many outstanding dogs that lived in homes as members of the family and there will be many more. I also firmly believe that the old dogs, or "Geezers," as we refer to them, deserve relaxed, comfortable lives after all their years of service. Put simply, that means a good home.

When Gretchen delivered a nine-pup litter after being bred with Mich — five girls and four boys — one boy stood out: he was the biggest, the strongest, the first to feed; he slept the least and pushed around the others the most. We didn't want this dog to leave The Line; he looked like he was integral to its future. Gretchen was descended from Cent and P.J., the outcross from New York, and Mich was, of course, a Jäger-Cent pup. So this little guy was from Cent on both sides, a product of what we call line breeding. This usually exaggerates the strengths of a line in some offspring and exaggerates the weaknesses of a line in others. Line breeding is much more common in England and Germany than it is in the United States.

We began to plot how we could keep this special pup in The Line. We couldn't really keep any more dogs at our house due to pet ordinances. We could send him to the club as a last resort, but the best idea by far was to get him into my friend Jim Miller's house where he could be developed as a great talent and breeder. The problem was that Jim Miller's house had a gatekeeper who would ultimately make the decision: his wife, Ann.

Ann was born in Canada, but she spent most of her life in the States. She's fun and loves dogs, kids and good times. A mother of three, she had an aging golden retriever who was as much pet as hunting dog. She knew it was time to replace Molly, but her inclination would be to do it with another golden. We simply invited them over to the house for pizza and never even mentioned the litter that was crawling around in the large upstairs bathroom and certainly not a whisper about a big, beautiful male that dominated the litter. We laughed, talked and chitchatted for an hour before we ever even broached the topic.

"Where's Gretchen?" Ann finally asked. As innocently as possible, "Upstairs with her litter."

"Puppies!" Ann exclaimed and we all moved quickly upstairs. Ann stood in the center of the litter with the little poopers scurrying all around her, and then in the confusion her eye caught sight of a big rambling ball of brown fur that even at that young age radiated purpose. She leaned over, grabbed that mass of potential and began to talk to him like an old friend. She didn't set the puppy down the rest of the night. She held him even while she was eating her pizza. From that moment on, there was no question who was going to be the Miller's next dog.

She named him Wilhelm in honor of me, but to the world he was Willy, and he became the strong, roaming, instinctive hunter he was bred to be. He was the kind of dog who could get you spitting mad because of his determined persistence to chase a deer or coon for hours; the kind of dog who would swell your head with pride as he would win tournaments or float effortlessly across the prairie as he pursued prairie birds in season. He grew to be 80 pounds of solid muscle, and his good-looks and talents excited observers. Willy gave The Line a way back to Cent and all of his powerful traits. At this time we held an embarrassment of riches: Willy, Mich, Mich's son Mitch and soon there'd be Fritz — all males who would strengthen The Line.

I had never before promised anyone (not even myself) a title or a victory. As a longtime competitor, I knew there were just too many things that can happen or go wrong. And yet, without prodding or prying, I predicted victory.

"Ann, I promise you that we'll have a State Championship on him by the time he's two!"

At the time, there were so many great dogs competing that the promise was especially foolhardy and frankly unnecessary. Willy was already six months, showed great promise and Ann loved him completely, but he was only a pup, not even out of training.

"Yep, I just feel it. I know he's going to be great," I said. Still, on our team alone, we had great talent like Mitch, Mich, Gretchen and Liesel. Liesel was from the last Jäger-Cent litter ever born; there had been only three dogs in that litter and she was the fastest learner, had the quickest eye and achieved by far the most in tournament hunting. She was lean and fast with a nice disposition. All these dogs any smart handicapper would put in front of the upstart Willy. Nevertheless I was confident of my predictions.

At Willy's first State Championship, I was not pleased with the way the older dogs were performing. So like a hockey coach might, I decided to mix up the lines on that cold January morning. Willy had only competed once before, but he'd shown promise. His retrieves were weak, but his bird finding was excellent.

"Okay," I said to the team that was underperforming so far in the event. "We're going to do everything different. Instead of me, Randy and Mich, we're going with Bruce, Willy and me in the next run."

No one argued. A few heads shook, but I was captain of the pointers; Randy was captain of the flushers, so mine was the last word here. Randy was a hockey player, so he knew exactly what I was doing. He had also become my partner at the Minnesota Horse and Hunt club, after he bought out Corky's interest. He was born in Canada and played Junior A before playing for the University of Minnesota–Duluth.

He had even won a Memorial Cup.

In his first-ever Open Class run, Willy charged into the field and Bruce and I followed him, like disciples. We harvested our birds in eight minutes; he retrieved them just fine. Willy won his first State Championship that day at ten months old — 14 months sooner than my braggadocio promise to Ann.

From the beginning to the end of the run, I felt the excitement that only comes when you get to perform with the great ones. Over his career, Willy won numerous titles and championships, and he was a threat to win every time he entered the field.

At this point The Line needed strengthening. There had been two huge disappointments. When Gus was born, he was also a large, beautiful male, deep brown with a strikingly gorgeous head. He was the pick of Jäger-Cent's third and last litter. It wasn't until he was six months old and all our hopes had been invested in him that we discovered he was cryptorchid, meaning only one testicle dropped. To most lines this wouldn't matter, but to us it meant that Gus would never be the stud dog we had dreamed him to be. We felt that we had worked too hard to introduce this potential deficiency into our breeding program. Gus was neutered and he lived life as a fine pet and working dog, until he was 13 years old. This further opened the window for Willy's breeding future and his role in The Line.

Gus's litter mate Liesel would become a great tournament dog and we would breed her to Mich's son, Mitch, in hopes of producing our next great stud dog. When Mixx was born, he too was the pick of a fabulous litter with Cent on both sides of the pedigree. He grew to be dark, tall, strong and very athletic, though Mixx never developed into the stud we expected.

Willy would sire several litters and throw as good as he was. For over five years, Willy, Mich and Mitch would be the standard bearers for The Line, taking things forward as we strived for better and better dogs.

THE KENNEL

Every day in a good kennel begins with the all-important cleaning, washing and disinfecting that sets the tone of the operation's priorities. In between the morning and early evening cleaning rituals, the dogs are exercised, socialized and trained in field skills. While the routine is repetitive, dogs thrive on consistency. The kennel dog's life lacks much of the human interaction and warmth that a well-placed house dog enjoys, but it can be a comfortable, clean, well-cared-for existence with a guaranteed full stomach and, in our case, good training and chances to hunt as a professional hunting dog. The forays into the field while guiding hunts become the highlight of the dog's life, its opportunity to interact with humans and the chance to gather praise dogs love.

When dogs don't have an activity, they sleep. It's actually amazing how much dogs really do sleep — sometimes 16 or more hours per day, and this increases as they age.

There have been some key people who have run the kennel over the years and made huge contributions to The Line in the process. Mike Chalupsky, who hid Rusty from me, was a good dog trainer and a central decision-maker on matters of genetics and breeding for The Line. Jan Munson, who eventually partnered up with Mike and moved with him to South Dakota, also brought in some major new bloodlines and innovative ideas as kennel manager.

Tory Martin managed the operation and made her own contributions. When she met longtime guide and dog trainer Mike Kretsch, they, too, merged and created a doggy daycare business and kennel down the road, keeping seven dogs of their own — some shorthairs, Labs, even a coon dog.

A wonderful guy named Mike Ahlgren ran the kennel for a couple of years and he brought an intellectual and thoughtful perspective to the job.

"Doggy John" (as we call him) has been with us a long time and he keeps the kennel clean and walks the dogs as reliably as a Swiss clock. He arrives for work an hour early every day so he won't be late and watches over the health of the dogs and pups. John is an uncomplicated fellow who loves dogs and they generally love him. If it's raining, he walks the dogs; if it's snowing, he walks the dogs; if it's hot and humid, he walks the dogs. He is always sensitive to conditions, but he is never deterred. Today Andrew Barbouche has been an important addition and strategist for The Line, as well as a good tournament player.

When we were starting in business, we didn't have the

same standards for cleanliness that we have now. Today we have cement facilities with cinderblock walls, well-designed drains and gutters, so it's much easier to keep it clean and sanitary than in the old days. Wood walls, wood door frames and wood fences collect germs and over time lead to inevitable problems. Kennels, not unlike schools or hospitals, are germ factories. With new dogs coming and going all the time, various diseases parade in. Kennel cough, parvovirus and coccidia all need to be caught early and eradicated often. When allowed to catch hold, they can spread quickly and threaten a dog's life or endanger an entire litter — or even the whole kennel.

In the early years we lost dogs and puppies to parvo and coccidia. Unfortunately, The Line lost over a dozen pups to each of these killers. It was with regret and sadness that we would bury those pups, but we would always try to learn from the experience and increase our protection.

Blastomycosis is a fungal infection that affects dogs as well as humans. It is caused by the fungal organism blastomyces dermatitidis, which is found as a mold in the soil and as yeast in body tissue. The mold occurs in sandy, acid soils in close proximity to river valleys or other waterways. It can create a variety of respiratory, eye and skin lesions. Blastomycosis can be rapidly fatal if not diagnosed and treated promptly. Even with proper treatment, many dogs do not recover from the infection. Along with proper medications, good supportive care is very important because the disease can wax and wane, improving slightly and then worsening again.

Mixx was born to be the next great breeding male in The Line. He was the son of Liesel (Jäger-Cent) and Mitch (Mich-Chelsea), so he was Jäger-Cent on both sides. Chelsea was a very good hunting dog, but most importantly she threw great dogs, especially tough-weather resistant, cold-nosed dogs. Mixx was handsome, precocious and quick to learn. We had been disappointed by beautiful Gus's cryptorchid condition and the tough decision to neuter him and move him out of the gene pool. Mixx, on the other hand, was no disappointment at all, being healthy, strong and on his way to becoming a great hunter.

He was now in his second year and ready to take his place in the field. We had hunted grouse and he was very promising when he suddenly fell ill. The fever was severe, the loss of appetite complete and his weight dropped quickly as a result. When the vet showed us the x-ray of his lungs, we understood how bad things really were. The lungs looked like they were filled with cobwebs; the fungus had overtaken them and Mixx was slowly suffocating. Meaner than pneumonia, the fungus was in control. As Kath is prone to do, she consulted with her medical friends Dr. Nancy and Nurse Mary Jo, and they determined that this fungus was not much different than the toenail fungus humans get on a rather common basis. At the time, itraconazole was a new treatment that was being used on humans for just that problem, so with little to lose the trio decided to try it. We gave Mixx doses of the drug intended for humans and we force-fed him rice and venison burger. Sure enough, within weeks he was significantly better. It was all working!

The thing that makes blastomycosis so tough to conquer is that the fungus has the ability to retreat into a remote part of the body and then, when the treatment stops, remount its assault. Over the course of a year, Mixx survived three separate counter-attacks. Even as he would appear to be healthy and out of the woods, he would in short order be stricken again.

A full year after his first contracting the disease, he seemed to have beaten the problem. As a celebration of his regained health, I took him hunting. He moved beautifully that late fall day, reminding me how exciting he really was. My hopes soared as I saw the perfectly built 75-pound muscleman knock down cattails and cover ground effortlessly. This was the dog that had been so near death that several nights we expected to find him dead the next morning.

As we hunted that day there was no question of his strength, vigor or mobility, yet he didn't find any birds. Sometimes that happens when you go hunting, I reassured myself, though I knew this was a very good area for birds. As the day went on, I saw a pheasant on the ground with my own eyes and moved to the bird, calling Mixx to join me. With the wind blowing strongly in his nose, I saw him run right by the bird, oblivious to its existence. I called him back around, but he again showed no sign that he knew it was there. On the third pass I came to suspect what would prove to be true. While the treatment had cured his disease and saved his life, its side effect was to destroy his ability to smell, and I now had a gorgeous three-year-old house pet that couldn't smell a thing. He would never be the hunting dog I had dreamed of and never take his place as a breeding male in The Line. The itraconazole that cured him had cost over $5,000 and the surgery to neuter him another $500. He was now the most expensive non-hunting dog I would ever own.

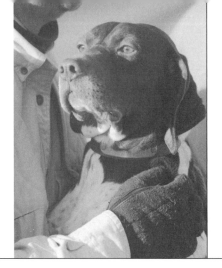

OTTO

As Mich had aged some, Bruce had every right to ask for another dog according to our deal. I'd supply him dogs for life, which he would care for and Kath and I would have the competition and breeding rights. The choice was a German short-hair pointer named Otto and he seemed to have all the right stuff. He was eight months old when Bruce got him; trained in the basics, Otto was fast and strong. The two got on well together, but there wasn't the same chemistry that Bruce had enjoyed with Mich right from the beginning. Otto was an outcross male, a bit of an experiment, but one we all agreed was worth trying. In other words, he was not genetically tied to our line, but his offspring would be because we'd planned to breed him to females from The Line.

Within weeks Otto had become "The Ottman" and his new name was used as much as his real moniker. We were all excited when the state championships came along and The Ottman could show his stuff. The Friday night before the tournament, Kath, Bruce and his wife Lori and I met up for dinner and stayed at the club. At about 8:00 p.m., we let the dogs out to leak and poop. The temperature had dropped throughout the day and now was near minus five degrees Fahrenheit and still falling. After about five minutes or so, most of the dogs were scratching at the cabin door, hoping to get inside by the fire. The aging Cent was missing, but the minute I stuck my head outside and called him, he came running in.

"Everybody accounted for?" Bruce asked.

"No, The Ottman is missing," Lori said.

We began to call out the door, but no response, so we all bundled up for bitter cold and went off to find Otto. Bruce drove to the kennel about a quarter mile away, always a likely haunt for a missing male dog. Kath and Lori walked on the horse trails, calling for Otto as they went, and I headed toward the other lodge and the garbage dumpsters, another likely spot. As I went I called for Otto, but I got no response. I checked every probable spot and then asked some guys outside the other rental lodge, where there was a party going on. They said they hadn't seen anything. After a 40-minute search I was frozen and there was still no sign of Otto. Expecting that the others had probably found him, I headed back to the cabin. We all arrived about the same time and no one had found Otto. At this point, we were worried.

We warmed up briefly and headed back out. The cold air grabbed our various voices as we split up and called for Otto. I repeated my search course, but again I was disappointed —

no sign of The Ottman. Then I approached the other lodge again. I went up on the porch and could see through the windows that the partiers had some porn films running on the TV. I knocked and they answered. Recognizing me, they asked, "How can we help?"

"Can I come in for a minute?" I asked.

"Sure."

As I stepped in I yelled, "Otto, here. Otto, here," and he came bounding toward me, down the steps, past the partiers, past the television and its blue movies. He jumped up on me.

"How long has he been here?" I asked.

"Oh, an hour at least," one guy said.

"Yeah, he's had two hot dogs and hamburgers," another guy said.

"And he sure likes to watch TV. I think he lay in front of that television at least 15 minutes," a third fellow chimed in.

Otto was found. He had crashed a stag party, came away with a full stomach and all of us were relieved to have him back.

When he was about two years old we sold The Ottman to a good hunter who would hunt him to 14 years, a rarity. He was never a key dog to The Line, though, because he had learned to fight. We bred away from that quality, so Otto was out. Those are very lonely decisions when all the talent and the great qualities are there, but something is just wrong. Bruce gave up and so did I.

MISTAKEN IDENTITY

Years later Mich would breed two great dogs, Fritz and Axel. Fritz would live at the club his first four years, getting trained and working as a professional hunting dog. His cold nose and natural skill would be obvious early on. Axel would live at Bruce's house. At seven months, Bruce brought him out to the club for training. He developed well and his talent was obvious. I was working out of my office in Montreal when I got the call that Fritz was missing. We had never had a dog stolen, so it seemed very odd. I listened carefully as I was told, "Fritz is missing and we can't figure it out. He was in his kennel an hour or two earlier, it was time to get him out and work him and he was gone. No one has seen anything; we're all on the look-out," our trainer,

Terry, told me. There was nothing I could do except worry. Of course, I'd been through a lot of this in my life, going back to me and Big Al repatriating numerous dogs in South Minneapolis — and Duke, of course. Later we went through the Dirk the Dog incident, so I had hope for Fritz.

Three days later, Bruce called me from up North. "I've been grouse hunting up here and I want you to know that this Axel is the best dog! He's findin' birds, retrieving and can he cover ground. You've got to let the guys at the club know they've done just a great job with him."

"Wow, that's good to hear," I said.

"There's just one thing we've got to work on," Bruce added. "He doesn't respond to his own name, which surprises me, but that'll come. Well, I've got to get back to the field, but I thought you'd like to know." He hung up.

About ten minutes later I picked up the phone and called the club. "Kennel, please," I said to the receptionist.

"Kennel, can I help you?"

"Yes, this is Bill. I was wondering if there's any news on Fritz."

"No, nothing, Bill," was the answer.

"Say, could you check and see if Axel is there?"

The phone went silent and then the voice said, "Axel is here. He's doing well, too. Looks real good."

"Okay. By the way, don't worry about Fritz any more. He'll be back tomorrow. When Bruce comes back from grouse hunting, he'll be out to return Axel, the dog who doesn't know his own name."

The kennel manager was a little confused, but he said, "Okay, I won't worry anymore."

Two years later, Axel *would* disappear out of Bruce's

kennel in his yard. It was a total mystery. Months later a neighbor came to Bruce and said, "Bruce, I don't know where to start, but I've found Axel. A friend of mine who is mildly retarded saw him at your house this winter and fell in love with him. He stole him out of your yard and brought him to his house up north. I went up to visit him last week and walked into his house. Well, there was Axel as big as life. I told the guy that what he did was wrong and the guy, of course, will give you the dog back, but Bruce I feel just terrible. What do you want to do?"

Bruce was as astonished as I was. Axel was supposed to be a key part of The Line — he was the son of Mich, grandson of Jäger and Cent, a great talent. Bruce and I talked about the situation and then we discovered that this guy had neutered the dog. He no longer had the same role in The Line and so we let the guy keep him. Axel lived out his life with the thief who loved him. I've never felt good about it, but I really didn't know what else to do and neither did Bruce.

MR. CENT AT 10

I had packed up the dogs and off I went on a hot August day. Jäger, Cent, Gretchen, Gus and Liesel, all kenneled up and ready for a trip. We were headed down to Heron Lake, Minnesota, to see a horse show and catch up with the gang down at the farm. Jan and Duane would meet up with me; Jan is the granddaughter of my godparents, Uncle Art and Aunt Jeanette. Alan — the guy who gave me my first "riding lesson" — is her father. We caught up with each other and watched Kath compete her thoroughbred. In those days Kath's knees were still good and she was a very good rider, jumping three-foot fences and higher, having a ball doing it.

The dogs loved the festivities and while they couldn't all be out at once, the excitement of a big event brought out the best in them. As always, people would comment on how beautiful Cent was, how handsome Gus was, how pretty Liesel and Gretchen were and how cute the one-eyed dog was. When the show was over, we all went off to a shallow river basin that Jan and Duane knew to let the dogs get some exercise. The hot, humid day made the water welcome for everyone and I threw dummies into the river and into deeper pools so the dogs would chase them down. They loved this game and I had two dummies going to keep everybody churned up and excited. Gus had become very good at it and, of course, Cent was always good at it. Liesel had become very good at stealing the dummy from Gus after he did all the work and then she'd grab it to get the credit. Jäger and Grettie were both competitive, too, so there were dogs running everywhere. We played for over an hour in that beautiful setting, all of us having fun in the process. At one point Gus had swallowed so much water he took a break and peed for four minutes, which was quite a thing to witness. Finally, it was time to wrap up and I put the dummies away, kenneled the dogs and we said goodbye to Jan and Duane. Kath and I were in separate vehicles because of the horse show. As we headed back to the Twin Cities, we agreed by cell phone that we should stop and get some supper in New Ulm, which was about half-way. We ate and then continued our trip. As I drove, I heard Cent stir like a dog does when they're dreaming. Sometimes as they sleep dogs move their legs like they're running. After his stirring, he was quiet.

When I got home I unpacked the truck and opened up the kennels to let the dogs out. Gus and Liesel bounded out as always. Cent hadn't moved. I opened his kennel and shook him mildly to wake him. He was cold to the touch on this still-very-hot day. I then realized he was stiff. Mr. Cent Von Esterfeld had died somewhere between New Ulm and Minneapolis. He had died peacefully and seemingly without pain, fear or alarm. He had died in one of his favorite places — in his steel-reinforced kennel in his truck — after a great day in the country doing what he loved to do. His heart had failed.

I brought him to the big cooler that night, all bagged up and kept him there until I could get to the farm where I buried him in clear view of his favorite lake and the land he loved to hunt. The sign on his grave reads: "Cent Von Esterfeld — Born in Germany — Winner of Four State Championships. His sons, daughters and grandpups are some of the most awarded dogs in history. 'Mr. Cent 1984–1994.'"

Jäger would search for Cent the next several days. She became withdrawn and slept on her dog bed at night, but edged toward Cent's now empty bed. She was now without her pal, protector, and patron. At 10 years old she still moved quite well and would for another year or two. She was still carrying 23 pieces of lead in her head and was of course blind in one eye; she no longer had the 80-pound Cent to reliably run next to her on that blind side.

Usually when a dog leaves the pack, other dogs begin to use their space and dog beds within a couple of days. In Cent's case, no one touched his space or his bed for over two weeks. At that point, we mixed up all the beds as if to say, "It's a new game, and yes, Cent is gone."

Several years later, after a great day in the field with Jim Miller and at one of his favorite places, at about the same age, Willy died. It was very similar. The aging Willy was still vigorous and adventure-minded. He never seemed to suffer and did what he wanted to do up to his death, which also seemed painless and without fear. These two great males would be saved from the debilitation of old age, cancer, feebleness or organ failures. They passed on with the dignity we remember those two great dogs living their entire lives.

TOR AND MIA

Down in Iowa, the Herold brothers needed some new dogs. Mitch was aging at Matt's house and Tim's Brittany had gotten old.

There has always been a healthy rivalry between the Herolds, and despite their eight-year age difference, Matt wasn't generally deferential to his older brother, Tim. Matt still lived on the family farm they grew up on and with that came a certain stature in the family order. Tim was well-ensconced and successful in the concrete industry and was running a cement plant for a family business that thrived in a variety of states. While Tim was the more accomplished high-school and college athlete, Matt was no slouch, and now his youth was a bit of an advantage as they continued to hunt, roughhouse and adventure. We had become good friends and teammates since the early days that began with the Rusty incident, and they had both become top-notch tournament hunters.

They loomed over the litter like raptors assessing their prey. Below their well-over-six-foot frames scrambled a bunch of pups that were from the core of The Line. Mitch (a Mich pup) was the sire and Greta was the dam. The men carefully watched the social interaction and the activity patterns to see who was the most assertive, who would back down the quickest, which pup slept the most, which pup rousted the others. With a fishing rod, line and a bird wing, they would secretly test which pups had the most bird desire at this tender age. Matt had the advantage because the litter was at his house, but Tim would sneak up and watch the group with his experienced eye and his 15-year-old son, Zac, would weigh in as well.

As pick day drew near, the tension would mount as each of the brothers wanted to get the best dog. They wouldn't share thoughts, notes or ideas. Intensity penetrated their most routine conversations. It was as if they were playing a high stakes poker game and the pot had grown to Trumpish proportions. Their wives began to whisper behind their backs about how silly this had gotten and how the secret observations were even disturbing their sleep. Choosing a dog for the Herold brothers had become a heavyweight championship title fight, or a game-seven playoff, even though there would never be a finish line, a final determination or a method of claiming victory.

Litter picks are serious business for some people and for others it can be no more than the exciting day you meet your future dog for the first time. I've seen men in their sixties pick up their puppies — the 10th or 12th pup in their lives — with the same excitement as a little kid at Christmas. The responsibility of taking an eight-week-old away from its mother and littermates into a world it doesn't know and can't imagine is staggering. I've known people who just gaze at their new pups for hours, people who cuddle and cradle them until their arms fall asleep.

"If they weren't so darn cute, you'd probably kill 'em," is a saying because they sure can get in so much trouble! They will chew on shoelaces as you walk, they will chew throw rugs, doors, woodwork or anything that falls on the floor. The tiny critters can pee and crap so fast that even the most aware and quick masters and mistresses will often fail to reach them in time. Without their littermates to wrassle and fight with, they need new things to occupy their days, and to this end every living or non-living thing in their world becomes a playmate, a target, an imaginary enemy, a toy or a treasure.

A puppy can bring a smile faster than a good joke, a laugh quicker than a comedian and a feeling of wholesomeness better than a Disney film. For the most part, "pick day" is one of the most fun, enjoyable and memorable days a person or family will ever spend together. To the person who will open their heart and their emotions to the new member of the family, the tiny little one will reciprocate and give back all that it gets.

The two muscular Iowans circled the litter box like they were about to wrestle. They didn't know who would get first pick until they flipped a coin. They verbally shot lines at each other as fencers would parry in preparation for the moment. They hadn't discussed the pups, lest it would tip off the other as to which one might be best. They were careful to not even look at their "pick" in case it sent inklings to the other brother as to which one had caught their eye. There would then be some gamesmanship before the coin toss. There were five boys and four girls; one of the boys was very runty and white.

"I hope you don't take that little white one," Tim said tauntingly. "I've got him pre-sold for over two-grand!"

Matt smiled and said nothing.

They continued to circle the box, never stopping, never leaning toward or touching any of the pups. Then the coin appeared as Matt's five-year-old son, Nathan, brought the silver dollar into the room. With everyone holding their collective breath, the coin went into the air and Matt called heads. The flip was tails. Tim would have first pick. Matt was crushed! Now the world had spun out of his control — the pup he had dreamt of for nights might be swept out of the box and hauled 120 miles away where he might see it occasionally, but not every day like he had hoped.

"Don't look at it — for God's sake, don't look at it!" he said to himself. He remembered how his big brother had always gotten his own way. Eight years Matt's senior, Tim could toy with his brother at will. Tim was driving cars when Matt could barely ride a bike. Tim was dating pretty girls when Matt was afraid to talk to the other sex. Now with one wrong look he could give himself away and if Tim saw Matt's choice he might take the puppy Matt wanted.

"Well, it's your pick," Matt said closing his eyes.

In a grandiose way, like a game show host might handle it, Tim said "I, Tim Herold, with the first draft pick in the greatest puppy draft in history do hereby take . . .," and then he leaned over and picked up a brown-headed, liver-ticked female, the largest female in the litter. Everybody cheered as he held it up above his head, the pup almost touching the ceiling. It looked so small in his huge hands. His smile was complete, his choice final and no amount of money, cajoling or sibling empathy would cause him to relinquish this prize.

Matt smiled coyly.

He was so relieved, because the dog he coveted was the big, fat, large-headed fullback that pushed everybody else around, the one who piled into his mother's breast, bullied the whole lot and pointed at the wing on the fishing rod. It was the big male that had excited him and that he had feared losing to his older brother. With a grin as big as a pie plate, he reached into the box and grabbed the feisty, over-sized male and said, "There are two first picks in this litter . . . one is a girl, one is a boy. We both have first picks!"

Shortly after, Matt's son, Nathan, christened the big boy Tornado Schnormado, the kind of name that must have surprised the American Kennel Club and that a hunter wouldn't reveal to his buddies. Tornado would become Tor. Tim's son, Zac, at the same time, named the little girl Mia, and everyone went to bed that night very, very happy with the day's outcome.

Over the next several years Mia and Tor would become, not surprisingly, great hunting dogs. Mia would be a city dog who also hunted; Tor would become a farm dog who would rove the Iowa farm and the land nearby, hunting fur and varmints — part of his job year round — and pheasants each fall with phenomenal precision. He would develop one of the coldest noses in the history of The Line, right up there with Gretchen, Beau and Fritz. A nose so keen that on the foulest days, the windiest conditions, with the barometer falling and scent cones shrinking to the size of a dollar bill,

Tor could still find birds. Never fast, his thoroughness made him a tournament dog. His sister was faster and also had a great nose. Her tournament career would be legendary.

When Tor was about six years old, I pulled into their driveway, and as always he came running to meet me as I got out of my truck. Whenever I showed up it usually meant a good day for Tor because it meant we'd go hunting. As I looked down at him and the width of his back, I smiled and said, "By golly, Tor, you sure found the feed bag, didn't you?" He had gained at least 30 pounds since I'd seen him last.

"Well, Matt, if you're half as fat as your dog, you won't be able to walk out there today." He smiled and shook his head.

"Well, he's takin' up eatin' anything he can find and I can't keep weight off of him," Matt said.

As we hunted it was surprising how well Tor still moved despite his size. Matt got the weight down as the season progressed, but Tor never regained his "girlish figure," and even when he became "Dog of the Year," he was at least 15 pounds overweight. Mia took fourth place and had become exceptional.

When she was diagnosed with tumors at age seven, we all held our breath. The fear of cancer is always there for dog owners. Our dogs spend their lives close to the ground. They breathe air and drink water that is full of agricultural chemicals, pesticides and insecticides that are ubiquitous in the modern countryside. Many of these toxins cause cancer or tumors and growths. The surgery took several hours, but the prognosis was good — no cancer for Mia — the tumors were removed and she faced a bright future. Her next season would be her best.

THE BUMPKIN

Fritz lived at the kennel and had done so his entire life. He was now four and I like to get the kennel dogs into homes about that age. Fritz had become a likeable, hard-hunting, good-looking field dog who was now demonstrating himself to be one of the best tournament dogs around. He had been a guide dog and hunted professionally since he was nine months old. He had always learned well, but not necessarily quickly. He had no flash, but he was filled with substance. While some dogs would dash around a field impressing the viewers with style and speed, Fritz would move at half the pace with his head high. He'd catch a whiff and hone in on it with a unique purposefulness until he knew exactly where what he sought was hiding. The son of

Mich and Chelsea, he was a full brother, but not littermate, to Mitch. So he was "Uncle Fritz" to Tor and Mia. At 65 pounds, he was a tight little package and I wanted to bring him home. With certainty I knew that he would fit into the pack at the bottom of the social order. Liesel was on top: Fritz was the low-man to Gus, Mixx, Abby, Haley, Hank, Scent and every dog to live or even visit his kennel over the subsequent years. He was a bumpkin, a country boy caught in a fast-paced, driven, urbane-like dog society. He wasn't assertive, he was submissive. He wasn't polished, he was covered with straw — but whenever birds were involved or the chips were down, it was Fritz who would come through.

Not so many years ago it was possible to fly dogs with you on airline flights for reasonable amounts of money — around $75 — and without a lot of hassle. During that time I was working a lot in Canada and would bring Fritz along. He needed exposure to a bigger world. I had a good pet porter for his flight, his vet papers all in order and it was time to make Fritz an international dog. We checked in at the airport and off he went with the special dog escort. I proceeded through security to my gate. The flight attendant knew that the person in seat 2C had a dog on board and immediately welcomed me and began to chat about dogs in general. As we talked I could hear Fritz woof, woof, woofing resoundingly as he was placed into the heated cargo section. We continued to talk as he continued to make sounds of horror, fear and anxiety below us. His woofs were not the strong confident woofs of a dog protecting his turf; they were the questioning woofs of a dog lost or off track. The woofs were interspersed with the quizzical barks dogs make like, "Do you like me?"

spiced with yelps of "Please, boss, please help me!"

After ten minutes of chatting over the sonata that Fritz had created, everyone on the flight knew there was a dog on board. "Can someone please help that poor dog?" people began to say.

Louder someone repeated, "Can you please help that poor dog?"

"I wonder whose dog that is."

"How could someone do that to their poor dog?"

Fritz continued his variegated sounds and the stirring in the passenger cabin mounted.

The flight attendant who had been so kind, welcoming and chatty now returned to me and said, "Sir, there are a number of us who think you shouldn't be on this plane. Your dog is suffering and here you are in first-class comfort. Just listen to him!" Just then Fritz let loose his most pathetic howl to date, the kind that began to affect my cold heart.

"He'll settle down," I promised and tried to change the subject. "Pull away from the gate," I implored, but we sat there.

More call buttons were ringing and I could overhear the subject.

"They should arrest that man for cruelty."

"What he's doing is horrible."

"What a mean guy."

I was getting no support at any level from this jury. I was guilty and that was it. As we pushed back, Fritz lit into a new litany of canine complaint. I knew now, though, that it would take a full-fledged mutiny to stop takeoff and was certain the German shorthair pointer in steerage was just fine. Eventually the engine drowned out his pathetic sounds.

We didn't hear another sound until we landed. Then the cacophony was renewed. As I waited in the customs line surrounded by my fellow passengers, I was greeted with cold stares, scowls, scoffs and expletives. Once through customs, the formerly friendly flight attendant said, "People like you shouldn't be allowed to have pets," and she left while I went to find Fritz.

He was silent and as he saw me approach his kennel, his hind end was wiggling out of excitement. We entered the big city, he sat in the passenger seat for the first time and he seemed to like it. He looked around, saw the sights of Montreal, the cathedrals, the busy streets, McGill University. It was fall and he, like many dogs, could smell the turned leaves and the dying grasses, knowing instinctively that these smells preceded the greatest autumn smell — game birds.

When we got to my apartment, which was on the third floor of a "bread and butter"–type of apartment building, Fritz ran up the stairs, absorbing the urban odors as he went. There were two other dogs in the building. He knew it right away, and he paused by their doors, but he didn't mark. He quickly explored the small place, as dogs do, and found a favorite spot.

The next day we ran together and he was as proud as any dog in The Line. He had run with me before, but never alone. He was always second or third dog on my morning runs, or even worse, left behind altogether. Here he was number one and only! I set him up for the day to be left behind his first day alone while I worked. The landlord rang by noon to say that the dog hadn't stopped barking since I'd left. I raced to the apartment and found Fritz in front of a full floor-to-ceiling mirror barking ferociously at his own reflection. I watched in wonder as he concocted new looks and sounds to scare off the other dog. Once I taped newspapers over the mirror the ruckus was over; the landlord made it clear that Fritz was welcome, but he could never be alone in the apartment.

I returned to the office with Fritz in tow. I left him in the car and went to work. About 3:00 p.m. the parking-lot attendant called and said in a very French accent, that he was going "crazeee." "You must come and save me!" he said. I went down and as soon as Fritz saw me he was quiet.

"No, no, Meester. He was bark, bark, barking allwaze, I promise," the attendant said.

"Look, he's a good dog. Can you keep him in your little hut with you?" I asked.

"Okay, I can try it." So, out came Fritz. He joined the parking-lot attendant in the little hut and they were fast friends for as long as Fritz was in Montreal.

We'd go to the dog park, which was a completely new experience for Fritz, and he'd meet non-hunting breeds for the first time in his life. Pekinese, Chows, Scotties, Collies, Shepherds, Sheep Dogs, St. Bernards. He was becoming the most sophisticated bumpkin in the land. There was no pack and no social order. I was alpha, he wasn't, and that was it. If the newspaper fell off the mirror he would launch his attack against the other dog. Otherwise, life was calm.

When the weekend came we went hunting for Perdrix (Ruffed Grouse) in the Laurentian Mountains and he excelled at it. When we found some other hunters (four Parisians with a Québécois guide), I was a bit down at first because they told me they had flushed 23 birds that day. Fritz and I had found only nine. I thought, "How could those guys have found more than Fritz?" As we talked I realized they had found 21 woodcocks and only two Ruffed Grouse, so I was now feeling much better and very proud. The guide told me how the Parisians don't shoot woodcock until they take a crap, which the birds do when they rise. I asked why, and the guide explained that they roast and eat the whole bird, guts and all. I moved on, feeling no need to tell them I had seen nine grouse and shot four already.

It was late in the day, the sun had set. Fritz and I were near the SUV when he made a low growl. Then I saw it. Not 30 yards away, a big cat moved out of the woods across the road from me. Not less than 90 pounds, it moved with quiet confidence and no fear. It looked me in the eye as if it was deciding if I'd make a good dinner. Then it slowly ambled away. I made some casts of its prints, took some pictures and reported what I had seen. I was told that there hadn't been any mountain lions or cougar in Quebec for 100 years and that what I had seen was a lynx. "But thank you for checking in."

I had been hosting a weekly radio show for years in Montreal that aired for an hour on Saturday morning and an hour on Sunday morning. It was on MENZ radio and tied to *MENZ* magazine, where I was editor-in-chief. "Where the Adventure Never Ends" was our tag line, and we urged people to get out there and do something. We rankled spectators and urged participation. The show ran on a sports radio station, so many of its listeners were couch potatoes who watched way too much TV and consumed far too much chips and beer. I told my audience I had seen a mountain lion and the authorities were telling me I had seen a lynx.

"Lynx are 22-pound cats and their tails don't resemble those of mountain lions. I'm with dogs all the time in the field, and in seconds I can judge the weight of a dog within two pounds. It's part of my being." This is what I told my radio audience the next day. Within days, I heard from the authorities; they wanted to meet with me. After much verbal fencing I finally asked why the wildlife commission didn't want me to have seen a mountain lion. I knew there had to be a reason they were so resistant. "If you saw a mountain lion, I would have to commission a study for three years, at least, at a cost of $250,000, which is money I don't have in my budget." I was told. "Life would be better if you hadn't seen it."

His honesty made me drop the whole matter. Within years, of course, others would see mountain lions and my silence became moot. Fritz and I had found the first mountain lion in Québec for over 100 years. He was no longer the bumpkin.

JACK

Renting out dogs is not something we typically do, but we have done it on occasion, especially to good members. It's usually the South Dakota pheasant season in October that drives the requests.

Jack was a solidly performing, steady, slow-paced dog that most hunters loved to hunt behind. When Loren (a club member) picked him up, we made sure he understood that Jack was a kennel dog, not a house dog. He wasn't housebroken and he wasn't above jumping on furniture and beds.

"Feed him in your motel if you want, but when you go to bed it's best to put him in your truck in a dog kennel," was our stern advice.

"Okay," Loren said as he excitedly took Jack

off on their hunting trip. "That's what I'll do."

On the way out on their five-hour drive, Loren began to worry about whether Jack might be cold in the back of the truck, so he brought him up into the heated cab with him. Jack settled into the passenger seat pretty quickly, and whenever he woke up from his frequent naps, he'd give Loren a big kiss.

When they checked into the motel, Loren brought Jack into the room and fed him as we suggested. Then the two lounged on the bed in front of the television until it was time for bed. Both Loren and Jack fell sound asleep right where they lay. They slept soundly through the night and it wasn't until they woke at 8:00 a.m. that Loren would discover he'd never locked the motel room door. His wallet was gone, along with all his cash, credit cards and driver's license. They'd been robbed and neither one of them had woken up!

The morning was lost to police reports and questioning, instead of bird hunting, but by noon they were finally ready to go hunting. Loren and Jack hit the field by one o'clock and were into birds by 1:30. After two hours, Jack began to tire. Suddenly, he barfed right there in the hunting field. When he was finished retching, Loren found five one hundred dollar bills, his driver's license (in two pieces) and his credit cards (two destroyed and one quite intact). From that day forward Jack was known as Jackpot.

THINGS GO WRONG

On the South Dakota opener some years back I had four dogs — three champions and Mixx. He was the big, good-looking dog who had suffered from blastomycosis as a pup and lost his sense of smell as a side effect. Now most people never knew he couldn't smell, because he put on such a big show running around and backing the other dogs, which was his specialty. Just at quitting time, as the guns were about to be put away, my three good dogs (Gus, Liesel and Fritz) hit one of the weak points that I don't like to see — the kind that suddenly evolves into a porcupine fight. Mixx was on the other side of the field and never got a quill, but the other three were skewered. After an hour of pulling and cutting, I realized I was making little progress. I gave it up and drove the hour to Pierre where the vet had agreed to stay open. Sedating the dogs and pulling quills began immediately, but she made it clear that the dogs couldn't hunt in the morning. I had a group to guide the next day, so this news hit me like a ton of bricks.

As the hunt began at noon that Sunday, I entered the field with Mixx and two golden retrievers that I had rounded up and conscripted into service. Now, considering all the insults I had cast upon their breed over the years, I was downright shocked that these dogs would agree to be seen with me, much less help me out of my mess. I had called them "fire-place dogs." I told several of their owners, "If I ever get so old I can't hunt anymore, I might buy a golden." I had suggested one for my niece when she was a six-year-old girl living in L.A., because I knew the dog would never hunt. I've called them "swamp collies" and other derisive names. Now I was about to guide a group of paying, out-of-town pheasant hunters with two golden retrievers and Mixx, my German shorthair pointer who couldn't smell. The birds were thick and the hunt went well. As the day went on, we were closing in on our limit, but I knew if my regular dogs were there, we'd have been done already. The day before nobody could tell one shorthair from another, so they all praised the group for the spectacular results. With the goldens there were no "backs" for Mixx to show off because the retrievers, of course, just flushed the birds. At this point, by my official count, the swamp collies had flushed 34 birds, Mixx zero; it was more humiliation than a self-respecting pointing-dog man should have to take. As the last two birds were shot and our limit complete, the host of the group walked over to me and said, "Thanks, Bill. That was quite a hunt. Sorry about your other dogs getting hurt, but I have to admit that if they hadn't been injured, I never would have realized how much better golden retrievers are than the shorthairs. You know, I'd like to buy me a couple of dogs. Do you think you could get me a couple of goldens?"

I do believe that this incident was the most humbling experience that this pointing-dog guy has ever had in the field, and that somehow the species is cumulatively gloating over it. If only the porcupine had gotten all four dogs that night, the humiliation wouldn't have been so complete.

END OF THE FIRST ERA

Jäger had been everything one could hope for. She learned fast, retained well and she had a kindness about her that was remarkable, which she showed to adults and kids, as well as other canines. While her conformation was good, it wasn't excellent, so it took more effort for her to cover a field, but the extra energy required brought liveliness and excitement to whoever saw her run. Her nose was the best I'd ever seen of any breed and she had that remarkable ability to 'pivot' on it. As she raced, she would catch the scent and stop midstride, her nose not moving as her entire body would fly around to accommodate her unmovable nose. No one was ever too tired to hunt with Jäger because she gave you back energy as you went.

I've seen dogs sulk and feel sorry for themselves, just like people do, but I never saw any of that from Jäger when she was recovering from 23 pellets in her head from a shotgun blast and as she lay blind in one eye. For a year she had worn a large plastic cone around her head, a "party hat" as we called it, to keep her from scratching or getting more injured after her shooting. Her enthusiasm for life wasn't diminished by the huge cone on her head that constantly banged into things. She never hesitated to reenter the hunting fields despite the disorientation that came with the blindness or any tenderness from injuries. With reckless abandon she would charge into the tallest or thickest cover in pursuit of birds, once the vet gave the green light to hunt. Success came back to her immediately as if she hadn't lost over a year of competition.

As we would run together in the mornings — Cent, Jäger and I — we'd go as fast as ever, as far as we'd want with Jäger on the right and Cent on the left protecting her blind side. When Cent died, Gus would take up part of Cent's role as protector and he'd run with his mother. She was still hunting with Gus and Liesel at age 11 for native birds and while she once got lost and scared in a 320-acre switch grass field, the minute she was reoriented and out of that huge, thick, tall field of grass, she was right back at it without missing a beat.

That was her last big hunt though. I'd work her in more limited areas from that point forward — woodlots and smaller pieces of cover. I couldn't imagine losing her in a tall grass field or endless cattails — not that little "squirt" dog as we called her — because she deserved better.

When she was 12 we began to notice that her hips were weakening and it would cause her to fall on slippery surfaces.

More and more we'd use throw rugs to give her traction on the hardwood floors. Overall she was revered by the pack and always brought a smile to my face as she would run up to welcome me home, her cute little butt wiggling hello. The little squirt dog was always ready to welcome. The winter of 1996 came early and it led off with an ice storm. Jäger was now almost 13. The ice covered everything — the sidewalks, the stairs, the ground. Most importantly it covered the deck and stairs of the dog kennel making them treacherous. Sheer ice awaited Jäger as she jumped through the door to go into the backyard kennel to relieve herself. Her back legs were unable to gain any footing and she slid precariously onto her stomach, laying spread eagled with her hind legs splayed out and unable to recover. The expression on her face was not surprise, embarrassment or chagrin; it was a sense of hope-lessness as now the most routine tasks of life were suddenly beyond her grasp. There were some tumors, too, that had gone undiagnosed because we don't put old dogs through surgeries only to gain a few months. However, from now on she would have to be carried outside and carried back in because her rear legs wouldn't support the weight of this once great athlete.

It was within a few weeks that her spirit began to weaken and what we always know to be inevitable began to settle in. Jäger wasn't going to see the spring. "The dog will tell you when" is a phrase we've always believed in — with their eyes, their actions, their inabilities. With the loss of her rear legs Jäger was saying "when." For the first time ever her spirit was broken and she deserved better. Doc Bailey came to the house. Jäger lay in Kath's lap as comfortable as she could get. She got the little shot that quickly and quietly caused the life of one of the best little dogs I've ever seen to slip away. She would be buried in the spring, right next to Cent Von Esterfeld at the farm.

This letter was sent to the doctor who saved her life when she was shot:

> Dear Dr. Sillerud and all of Jäger's Friends:
> With still some sadness, but no regrets, I need to inform all of you that Jäger was put to sleep on February 5, 1996. We still long for her. She was doing pretty well through Christmas and actually went on a hunt in early January. When first the ice came and then the bitter cold weather hit toward the end of January, she just couldn't function. Even though she only had to venture outside to relieve herself, those hips just wouldn't carry her. So, we had no choice but to put her down. She got to see the litter of her "grandpups" that was born the end of January and she died at home in my arms. Jäger was cremated and soon will be buried next to her mate at the hunting farm we have in western Minnesota. We are left now with her four-year-old son and daughter and also Mixx, her eight-month-old "grandson" who will be making his first pheasant hunting debut soon.
> Thanks to you, Dr. Sillerud and your competent and caring staff, Jäger was given a second chance to fulfill an awesome hunting career. She never wanted or needed any sympathy or special treatment because the sight in one eye was gone. We came to a point in time that we got so accustomed to her blue eye it became part of her charm.

Thank you all again for helping a special little dog, and the family that loved her so much, through a near tragedy that turned to triumph.

Fondly, Kathy and Bill Urseth
Gus, Liesel and Mixx

THE LOST LAB

The black Lab was old, at least nine or ten, and was running along the highway looking confused. Then I noticed a second dog that appeared to be with it. It was December and it was cold. At first I drove past the dog, and then I realized that in 25 years of driving that road I had never seen a stray dog on it before, so something was probably up. I turned around and went back. I knew I'd be late for my meeting now, but somehow that confused Lab seemed more important. As I called him, he came quite quickly. I checked for ID and kenneled him up in my truck. There was no ID and the other dog wouldn't kennel, so I yelled "go home, go home" hoping I could follow him to his house. No such luck; after about a mile, the dog shagged me and I was left with the old, untagged black Lab in the truck.

As I would have done in the very old days, we started with signs and word of mouth and eventually contacted the local animal-control people. Once the "lost animal" people got involved, they brought in their own rules and policies, which I soon realized were pretty lethal. Their three-day rule was that any untagged dog not claimed within three days will be dispatched. Now, this didn't mean they'd be "dispatched" to some hunting camp in the Dakotas or a tony club outside Chicago. This meant terminated, euthanized, put down. What had started as a well-intended rescue mission had now put the old Lab on death row. Unless the owners found our signs in time, the game was up.

Then Kath swung into action and began to solicit other people who might want a dog, to agree to claim the dog as a last-minute reprieve. Sure enough, she found a couple who were willing, so with two days gone and the hours ticking down, the couple was ready to raise their hands and say "we'll take him." As three o'clock came close, the Lab's true owners wandered into the little corner tavern where some of our signs were placed. Thankfully, they called right away and with 40 minutes left on the clock, they reclaimed the old Lab and the dog was safe. We notified our Plan B participants and thanked them for their willingness to step up. It was not without some anxiety, but the world was right again.

ABBY

Her life began as a kennel dog. Abby, her sister Annie and her brother Ty were all key new members of The Line. They were all strong hunters and came on fast. My longtime partner, Rich Boumeester, took Ty. We kept Annie — who had great potential in everyone's mind — and Abby. Annie only grew to be 28 pounds — but she was quick, persevering and filled with bird-finding intensity. She stole everybody's heart, and I was hearing about Annie from every person I saw. They all came out of Sonne (a Mich pup), who threw fabulous litters, and an outcross stud out of Wisconsin. They were two generations from Jäger-Cent and were as quick to learn as Jäger herself.

Abby grew to be 52 pounds, with perfect conformation. She was liver-ticked and, because she was so well-built, she moved effortlessly. While Annie seemed to have boundless energy, it was her small size that made her seem so quick.

The first time I actually hunted them alone, I was impressed with Annie, whom everyone hoped I would love, but I was swept away with Abby. She was smart and looked you in the eye the way Jäger used to do. She was very cute and would always finagle herself as close to you as possible to sneak a kiss, a pat or a hug. She found birds with the certainty of her hot nose, but didn't blow by them like hot-nosed dogs are prone to do. She was only seven months old, but showed so much promise. As cute as Annie was, she wasn't going to be the strong, smart, athletic hunter her sister could become. Mike Kretsch, longtime guide at the club, began to use Abby on hunts and she quickly developed her own fan club. Guides count on tips to enhance their incomes, and Abby made the cash register ring.

After several weeks and some outstanding tournament performances, Abby had completely stolen my heart. Her athleticism was of the type that I had only seen in dogs like Mich, Willy and Cent, some of the best males from The Line. Her nose had the certainty that Gretchen's had provided a decade earlier, but she was so much faster than Gretchen or Fritz, who was the dominant nose in The Line at the time. Abby's personality was closest to Jäger's — the intense desire to please, the biddability and the cleverness to always be closest to her people. At dinner she'd rest her head on your leg under the table, not to beg but to be close. During cocktails, she'd sidle right up next to you and stand compliantly, shifting if you shifted, but never in the way. In the morning she'd rest her chin on your bed right next to your face and just gaze at you, never making a sound. She would come and "say goodnight" before she'd lie down on her dog bed, looking for a couple of pats on her head in the process. Everything about her screamed of disciplined, purposeful talent, and when she finally earned her way into the house after a year and a half in the kennel, she became head of the pack in a matter of days. Without a fight or even much growling, Abby eased Liesel out of her role and became the alpha.

Competing in puppy and professional categories at the same time, she would instantly dominate both classes under most conditions in tournament hunting.

Meanwhile, Abby's full brother and littermate, Ty, was her male counterpart, but the testosterone made him tougher and edgier. Rich Boumeester, my partner, had raised him early on; then we got him because Rich wanted to focus on his English pointers, and he had discovered a bit of a mean streak in Ty that concerned him.

When dogs begin to demonstrate that mean streak, the moments that precede and follow an incident are so important to reaching a peaceful outcome. Rich knew this very well and wasn't afraid or reluctant to "flip a dog" when it needed to be done. Flipping only works when you catch a dog *during the act* of doing something aggressive, and you must move on the event decisively. One takes the dog, flips it on its back and slaps the dog several times and chokes it until the dog is clearly submissive and knows who the boss is. From the process a dog should learn who's in charge and that their behavior won't be tolerated. The practice was initiated by wolves, and pack behavior still dictates the use of this primal method because it works. You don't need to beat the dog, just slap it some; you don't choke to kill, you choke to submit. A truly defiant dog will growl, nip and with their eyes communicate "I'm going to get you for this" while it's happening, but when it's over, it's usually just over. We feared Ty might be enjoying fighting too much, which can happen to dogs, especially when they win their fights. It has an invigorating effect and leads to more encounters unless you deal with it right away. Rich wasn't afraid to deal with it and when I got Ty back I wasn't either, but the objective of "flipping" is to never have to do it again after the first time.

The same toughness that makes a dog great in the field on a long day or the fourth day of a hunting trip can make some dogs bullies; separating these traits out is not easy, but it's essential.

One snowy morning when I had left Fritz and Ty outside together briefly, I returned to a full-fledged dog fight. Fritz, as a shy bumpkin, never fights. Ty's reputation preceded him, and since he was now on top of the passive Fritz, tearing away at his submissive senior, I went after Ty and "flipped" him. He was furious that I would assert myself and intrude on his ass-kicking of Fritz. He would try to roll and get off his back, but my weight and position wouldn't allow it. His growl was deep and ferocious, but the louder he'd get, the more I would squeeze his throat. His eyes communicated fear, not so much fear of me as the loss of position that this meant to his status in the pack. Fritz had always accepted his lowly position in the pack beneath Liesel, Gus, Mixx, Ty's sister Abby and Ty himself, but Ty would challenge anyone, perhaps even Abby herself, for dominance. Now I (as a new master) was pushing him down and simultaneously taking away a favorite form of recreation. After what seemed like an eternity, he would submit. I was now his alpha and he knew it.

I patched Fritz up. Some holes in his ears and a couple of other puncture wounds were the extent of his physical injuries. His psyche was another thing; he was now afraid of Ty and would avoid contact with him; never being aggressive or a bully himself, he just couldn't sort out Ty's behavior. As for Ty, he would not get in another fight for months and by then, my friend and partner, Andy Miller, had the dog. It was good to see this great talent in a good home again.

They were at a field trial where two dogs compete in the same field at the same time hunting for the same birds, one on one. Andy knew of Ty's background, but as we all did, he liked the way he hunted, with his phenomenal nose and go-for-broke attitude. At the line, he saw the hair on Ty's back go up and sure enough on the release of the dogs which began the hunt, Ty launched into the other male competitor like Brock Lesnar on a bad day. Despite his abject embarrassment, Andy threw himself into the fray, trying to save the other dog, submit his own dog and regain his now diminished status in his own pack. The 35-year-old physician would gain order out of the chaos, and once the order was achieved, Ty would be readily thrown out of the competition for his behavior. Andy's patience with Ty was largely due to his respect for the dog's undeniable abilities. All of us loved to hunt the dog on native birds or in competition, but we would all be careful and cautious whenever he was around another male dog. He never did bother females.

The following March we were all together at the Iowa State Championship. Iowa springs are muddy with melting snow and ice. On this particular Saturday it was raining, which made it even worse. Andy Miller has always been an even-tempered, accomplished kid, since I first met him at age three. We've hunted together since he was 12, and he's become a very good dog man and family practice doctor, but there is one thing that can send Andy's temperature flaring and that's "Old Ty." I'd never seen such a scrap since *McLintock!*, John Wayne's epic Western. Sure enough, Ty raised the hairs on his back, growled and made a move on this muddy day for another male competitor. Before Ty could even sink his teeth into the other dog, Andy jumped on him and they began to wrassle in the Iowa mud.

The scuffle went on for a good five minutes and our jaws dropped as we saw and heard the mild-mannered "life-saving doctor" call his dog every name in the book as he slapped, flipped and choked the dog into muddy submission. When Andy victoriously rose from the fray, it was so slippery he couldn't maintain his footing and fell, adding a little more mud to his already-covered body. A dozen earthworms could have lived comfortably on him, but Ty was compliant from the experience. Only Andy's white smile conveyed any brightness as he said, "By God, I hope he learned from that one!" We all hoped Ty had learned from that one, because all of us dog guys knew Andy did what he had to do. We also knew how easy it can be to not do what we need to do as masters.

A couple of days later, Andy called and said that he thought maybe it was time to neuter Ty. I still owned breeding rights and Andy was essentially seeking my permission. I readily agreed, but added that even though it would probably help, it might not solve the problem completely. Andy said he understood, but that it was probably the best shot. This would eliminate a great hunter from The Line, but it would be better to remove the fighting characteristic. We still had Abby and Annie, and they shared the same genetics. Ty hunted native birds, but his tournament life was basically over along with his future as a stud. Thank goodness, his fighting stopped. Several of the males he threw in his first litter, sure enough, would be fighters, too, and they were sorted out of The Line as well.

Abby was the alpha running the show and keeping the pack in order at home. Liesel submitted easily and they became pals. Gus, Mixx and Fritz were putty in her paws and Abby was number one. The doghouse roof was five feet high, and though it had a slight angle, it was basically flat. It was covered with shingles. The doghouse was used intermittently by the dogs as a place to recluse themselves from their pack mates, the sun, the cold or when they wanted a change of scenery from their kennel. Sometimes Abby would feel the need to demonstrate her position with the pack and she would, in a very athletic maneuver, jump up on the doghouse roof and then proceed to bark and strut back and forth to the howls and barks of her amazed minions, who would circle and occasionally try (but fail) to get up there themselves. The whole thing was reminiscent of Lawrence of Arabia strutting on the top of the Turkish rail cars after a successful raid. The adulation of the other dogs was palpable and, at times, in a dramatic movement, she'd tear off a shingle and toss it with her muzzle to her admirers, who would then chew on the shingle. It was a truly amazing feat. It was a stunt of dominance that I appreciated (up to the shingle-ripping), but it clearly reinforced her unchallenged position in the social order.

She had put together an impressive streak of tournament victories, winning at a state championship level and playing successfully at a national level. She reminded me of Jäger and was now the complete dog in the house, at the duck camp or in the tournament field. She was friendly and social, always sidling up to me in any situation, not in a pushy or intrusive way, but in a reassuring way. "Don't worry, boss. If you need me, I'm right here. Of course, if you want to scratch my ears, go ahead." She had a lifelong habit of waking up at 5:00 a.m., standing bedside and waiting until you woke — just staring and waiting. She had become the sweetest little ball of fire I had ever seen.

Abby was all the hunt and none of the trouble that Ty could be. She was breaking new records in competitions and winning the hearts of most who met her. Smarter than most dogs of our line, she also had that Jäger trait of looking a person in the eye. When it was time to breed her, we chose my longtime friend and competitor Ryan Stafne's dog Cowboy as the sire, believing that this would lead to biddable, strong, well-conformed hunters with lovable personalities — and it did. Cowboy was a very good hunter; lovable and biddable, he moved beautifully and was Ryan's dog and pal.

Abby was a predictably great mother and cared for her pups unselfishly right to the end, when at eight weeks they'd be sent off to their various new homes and families. We kept three, knowing this was a crucial key to The Line. Toby, Sieger and Maddy were the dogs that we were counting on to breed back to the core of The Line, the Jäger-Cent, Mich and Willy dogs we had so valued. Tim Herold would have Toby, Bruce would have Sieger, both with great tournament futures, and Maddy would be primarily for breeding, although she was an outstanding hunter herself. She would eventually go to club member Bob Monio who had two daughters that loved her very much.

Abby's second breeding would be with Tor, the big, sure-nosed multiple-champion down at Matt Herold's. Tor was the core of The Line with Jäger, Cent, Mich, Mitch — great dogs all in his background.

He had become a reclusive hunting machine, hunting coons, possums and skunks on Matt's farm for days at a time. Tor ate pig food and his weight ranged from 70 pounds of solid muscle to 95 pounds of solid something. His instincts were to hunt, his cold, sure nose allowed him to do it and his expanded size made him the top of the food chain in northern Iowa. We would all laugh when we'd see him because he would look so big and cumbersome, but then when he'd swing into action, all smirking would stop because he could really find birds. After being Dog of the Year, no one chuckled anymore about his waistline.

Because of Abby's second pregnancy, she was dealing with her own waistline issues at the 2006 U.S. Open. She was slow by just a step, but that was enough to cost her the championship, and her little cousin Hooty would win Dog of the Year. Shortly afterward, Hooty was pregnant herself.

Abby's second litter was healthy, happy and problem-free. Many waited for their pups with the anticipation inspired by top-bred litters. She would once again mother and nurse the litter with the care and concern we'd come to expect from this very special dog. While her litter was growing with predictable smoothness, things were not going as well for Hooty. Going into labor exactly eight weeks after Abby, Hooty struggled for 24 hours after her water broke without delivering any pups. When she arrived at the vet's office, they performed a Caesarean and discovered that five of the puppies were already dead and one had blocked the birth canal; her labor and struggling were for naught. The vet saved three sick and infected pups, but Hooty, Dog of the Year and cute as a button, would have a hysterectomy and be out of The Line after her first litter. She was so weak and stitched up, she couldn't nurse her pups, and now the three survivors were at risk of starving.

Earlier that day, Abby's pups had been given to their new families who waited for them. It was then that Kath decided to try something. She brought Hooty's puppies to Abby's box, slipping them in where her own pups had just lived. We both knew that this was either going to work or it could be a death sentence to the newborn pups. Mother dogs have the ability to sort out frail and weak pups with very little mercy. They kill them or throw them out of the nest. These pups were on antibiotics and were clearly not out of the woods yet.

Abby sniffed the pups and lay down with them immediately. They began to crawl toward her breasts, which she freely offered to them. They began to suck, and she nurtured them as Hooty lay in intensive care fighting for her life against the infection that had killed five of her pups and imperiled the other three.

After two days with Abby, Bernie and Rowdy, as they'd be named, had turned the corner, but the third still-unnamed pup was not gaining strength. Abby pushed the dying pup away to the benefit of Bernie and Rowdy. The pup died shortly thereafter. Kath would shed a tear, but she understood that Abby did the right thing since it looked like Bernie and Rowdy would live. Hooty was growing stronger and stronger, but she never saw her pups. She needed to build her own strength, and Abby had willingly become mother to the two survivors. In a few weeks, Hooty would be placed in a wonderful home, not far from the club, with a loving hunting family. Bernie and Rowdy would become beautiful dogs, quick learners and, Bernie especially, fine athletes.

Bernie was trained by the great Terry Holzinger, who can bring out talent like few can. Bernie led his obedience class and proved to be very sociable. His hunting was certain and confident.

HALEY THE CALIFORNIA GIRL AND GUS

Several years after Jäger was gone we began to seriously think about bringing on another dog to keep up the strength of The Line. We knew that we had bred The Line for hunt and we had consistently seen the results. They were gratifying and rewarding. When you always opt for hunt ability in your breeding decisions, there are times when you can get off track as it applies to conformation and maintaining standards to the breed, like height and weight type standards. While we never lost track of this issue, it wasn't usually our number one priority. Jan Munson, when she was running the kennel, was extremely sensitive to this issue and she sought out dogs to bring into The Line as outcrosses who were from show stock and had outstanding conformation.

Haley was just such an outcross that we found in California. While she never had to fly over the Atlantic to join us as Cent did, she did have a three-hour flight and we were very excited to meet her when she arrived. She was as gorgeous a dog as we expected, about 60 pounds (large for a female), perfectly proportioned. She was visually everything we hoped for. The concern with outcrosses that we buy for this purpose is, "can they hunt?" We rushed Haley into the field to see if she could. Within an hour any concerns were completely alleviated as we realized she could find birds, hold point, back, retrieve and work a field with confidence. With her excellent conformation she had great mechanics so she could float a field effortlessly, the way I love to see dogs move.

Haley was a soft dog who loved to be with people. She had lived in the kennel now for years, but as I got to know her better and better I realized that she would thrive in a home and her full potential might not be realized living in a kennel. At this time Gus and Liesel were aging and winding down. It seemed logical to bring Haley into the house and make her part of the pack, which we did. Her personality fit well because she never tried to usurp Abby who was the Alpha or Liesel who she had replaced. The rest of the boys were all submissive as well. At this point, the order was Abby, Liesel, Gus, Haley, Mixx, Bernie and, of course, Fritz who was very accomplished in the field, but socially still the bumpkin. Haley would begin to win tournaments and work at the Club as a professional guide dog and in the house, she blended right in.

I had been on the road for about a month. It was early August and I was packing up to go to Argentina to do some television shows. At this time I was starting in outdoor television with Trevor Gowdy, and we were doing a show called *In the Hunt*. Trevor is an outstanding television talent and producer. His father, Curt Gowdy, was still alive then and he did voice work for the show. Curt, of course, was the *American Sportsman* for 23 years, and he broadcast Super Bowls, World Series, Olympic Games and *The Wide World of Sports*. He was the best of his profession.

My hunting gear was in storage in the garage — the camouflage clothes, waders, calls, all the gear that Gus associated with the thing he loves most, duck hunting. Gus had been pulled out of breeding early on when he came up cryptorchid, but he had become a phenomenal retriever and could work ducks with all but the best of the best Labradors. He was ten now and had diminished some, the effects of cold water and the resultant arthritis having exacted a toll from his svelte body and oily coat. When he saw me going through the duck gear, he became puppy-like and animated.

"Oh boy, boss, this is it! We're goin' huntin' — just you and me and the ducks." His tail wagged as these thoughts seemed to bounce out of him. He sniffed every article of gear I laid out with approval. Walking amongst all the equipment, he seemed to rule over the event. The other dogs lay in the kennel. Being upland dogs they found this procedure much less thrilling than Gus did.

With the gear all over the floor, I inadvertently hit the garage-door button and the mechanical door began to open. With the speed Gus had lost several years earlier, he bolted for freedom and charged toward The Big Swamp down the hill from the house. This is a 60-acre thick cattail slough — most of which the club owns — and is used for its sporting clays courses. To Gus this was duck country, and because it was a sporting clays league night, there were hundreds of people out shooting shotguns; these sounds fed Gus's hunting fever. I ran after him yelling, "Gus, Gus. Come here, Gus," but he would have none of it. Stoked by the visuals of the gear, the gunshots, the cattails and the ducks he was chasing off to The Big Swamp. He was on his own mission.

I ran down and into the water calling and calling and began to move toward where I heard Gus's splashing and where I saw birds rising. On the hill above me, the sporting clays shooters were firing their shotguns at clay targets over my head, and the broken targets were raining down on me. The cattails were so tall they couldn't see either Gus or me as they shot. Finally, I realized I needed to withdraw; the shooting was too intense. I raced back up the hill and jumped in my truck to continue my search from the sporting clays course on the right side of the guns.

The Big Swamp is an unforgiving place. It's thick and difficult to orient in. Gus was at an age where he could become confused and physically tired. No longer in the shape he was once in, he was also in danger on a hot night like this of having a heart attack like his father Cent and cousin Willy did after wild romps at the same age. I raced along the course asking every group, "Have you seen my dog? He's out in The Big Swamp. Right in front of you, down there," I would point to where I thought he was. The fourth group included an old friend.

Cal looked at me and said, "Yes Bill, I saw him. He was right out there." He pointed where I had heard Gus last. "He was barking, then he was woofing, but finally I heard him howl and go quiet. I think he's dead. He never moved again from that spot."

I went home soaking wet, full of mud. It was dark now and Kath had to be brought up to date. All she knew was that he was missing and she sat on the swing outside weeping. I approached and told her what I had learned. Then I said, "I think he's dead." She sobbed deeply and said, "You've got to find his body."

I don't fear swamps like many people do. Some of my fondest memories are in cattails and mushy bottoms, but finding a dead dog in a cattail slough in August at night is an impossible task, not one even the most ardent swamp rat would take on successfully. She kept repeating, "We've got to find his body. We've got to find his body."

I was scheduled to go to Argentina the next morning and knew that it could be a two- or three-day task to find the dead dog and that's if the birds helped. It was clear, however, that what was haunting her most was that Gus was missing, not that Gus was dead. Her grief ran deep for the next hour.

At 9:45 p.m. the phone rang and Bob Burditt at the club was on the phone. "Bill, the old dog is here at the check-in. He looks pretty tired. Can you come and get him?"

I was silent for what must have been 20 seconds, taking deep breaths and absorbing the news. Finally I said, "I'll be right there."

Gus was tired and worn from his jaunt. He had emerged from the swamp when the shooting stopped, made it to shore and then to the familiar check-in he knew so well. He had stood by the door until they let him in. They cleaned him a little, but he was still mud-caked when I saw him. I was mad and happy, split by contradictory emotions, but I understood that he wanted to go hunting with me and that he needed to demonstrate that to me loud and clear. The next morning

I'd get up early before my flight to Argentina, and Gus and I went alone for about two hours through hills, fields and swamps. We spent some quality time together. I was told later that he slept most of the next two days.

BERNIE

Bernie's first hunt with me was duck hunting out west at Long Tom Farm. It was cool, but not cold. I picked up Abby's adopted pup from the club kennels that weekend. I was so proud of what I knew would be my future stud dog and champion. All indications were that he would be the natural successor to the great ones in The Line. On his first duck hunt, he showed strong desire. He marked and he retrieved birds well. I was pleased; at only seven months it was more than I could hope for. The second day we went to a different slough, which was much more difficult and involved sitting in the water and waiting for ducks. Bernie kept shivering and getting out of the water. I was very disappointed. When we walked back to the truck he crawled into the front seat when I wasn't looking and barfed all over the floor of the truck. I was concerned because I couldn't explain why he was cold and now sick.

His health would diminish over the next month and then the diagnosis would reveal he was suffering from renal failure — his kidneys were failing. There was nothing we could do for him but make him comfortable. It pained me to look at him — so beautiful and well-marked, so strong and handsome, most of all so pleasant and nice to be around. Abby, as head of the pack, had nurtured him, weaned him, taught him, molded him socially and even disciplined him into something special, and he was dying. The pack at this time included the "old dogs" Gus and Liesel; Haley, who was a beautiful four-year-old female; Fritz, the simple but very talented hunter; Mixx, the dog who had no sense of smell; Bernie; and, of course, Abby.

They slept in a big pile on dog beds and the seven got along very, very well. They had a big run and could go into or out of a heated indoor kennel; they could hunt and exercise on the club property almost every day and they had people who really cared about them.

Strangely few of them were now key to The Line itself. Haley had a good breeding future and threw very good dogs. Fritz was a stud and Abby would still, at seven, have one more litter, but Gus could never breed, Liesel was past her breeding years, Mixx could never breed and now Bernie was out of The Line. If it weren't for the teammates Matt Herold with Mitch and Tor, Tim Herold with Toby, Bruce Wohlrabe with Mich, Beau and Sieger, and Jim Miller with Willy — some of the The Line's greatest dogs — The Line might have ended due to bad luck and space limitations. Because of these guys and their wives and kids and the great homes and care they gave the males of The Line, it would prosper, and the dogs would continue to be socialized, trained and nurtured.

CHARLIE
OF THE EXTENDED LINE

After the Buster incident my sister let a few years go by before she was ready for another dog. Emily, my niece, was about four years old. She was precocious, bright and fun, and I wanted her to have the dog I never had as a kid. Kath and I never had children. Bonnie and Gerry only had Emily, and Gerry had no brothers or sisters, so this is one small family, and Emily had a lot of adults who really cared about her. Theirs would be a non-hunting household and I never even considered a dog from The Line as a nominee for the job. I strongly endorsed the idea of a golden retriever, which I believe is one of the prettiest, best-tempered breeds on earth. We found some breeders in Western Minnesota who seemed to have just the ticket: a well-bred, good-tempered golden retriever with good hips and hunt optional. We all drove to see the latest litter with no obligation but open minds. Emily wanted a dog and everyone wanted her to have one. The holidays had brought them to Minnesota, and I was confident our breeders would be more reputable than any in California.

We liked the people right away, then we saw the litter. The mother was a caring, good-looking golden with a red hue that I found appealing, and most importantly, so did everyone else. Because the dog wasn't going to hunt anyway, I never asked to see her or the sire in the field, something that I do when looking at a hunting dog. Then, I always do a field check and watch how the older dogs move.

The litter was predictably cute — alright, downright beautiful! The puppies instantly stole our hearts and compromised the scrutiny that should precede with a 12- to 15-year commitment and a $15,000 to $20,000 investment.

Simply put, the price a person pays for a dog is a pittance compared to what a dog costs over its lifetime. The normal dog lives 12 to 15 years and costs about $1,200 per year to keep. It breaks down to $400 per year for food, $400 per year for vet and health, $400 per year on accoutrements such as leashes, dog bones, kennels, collars, training, training collars, toys, dog beds, portable kennels, clothing, licenses, fees and the list just keeps going. As a result the average dog can easily cost $12,000 to $15,000, and this estimate is only accurate if you have no serious health issues, you never show, compete, field trial or tournament hunt the dog. Then all bets on costs are off. That's why you should never try to save money on the purchase price of a dog. The price difference between $400 and $1,000 for a top-notch puppy is nothing and will be made up on training expenses alone.

Emily chose her pup and named it Charles. It would soon be Charlie to most, Chuck to some, Charles to me. As I held and reviewed this gorgeous, furry little creature, I found myself imagining a completely different future than I would for a dog from The Line. I pictured this dog in a fenced-in suburban backyard, rarely seeing anything else in its life. I saw little kids playing with it, pulling its tail, riding on its back, swimming with it in the swimming pool. I saw it living indoors and lying amongst its favorite people most of the time. I didn't see long road trips to distant locations or skunk, coon or porcupine fights. I never pictured days afield in strange never-before-seen or -smelled countryside in dozens of different states. I never worried about conformation, that mysterious quality that determines how well an animal can float through a field. When I look at our pups I want to see some scrap, some determination, some fight — not a mean streak, but some fight. With Charles I wanted to see love and affection. It was a different day, but very exciting as puppy picks are.

Back in Los Angeles, Charles settled very much into the life I had pictured for him, not due to me, just because, in fact, these were the stuff of his life: swimming pools, kids' parties, suburban backyards, a loving family. On one of my visits, I stopped by between business meetings to see everybody and check out how "the Extended Line" was doing.

At only two years old, Charles was limping noticeably. He favored his right hip. My sister had noticed, but I'm not sure that anyone else did. When we were alone I said, "Have you had his hips done yet?"

"No, not yet," she responded. She tightened up her jaw and neck as she said it, the way she did when she was a kid and there was more to the story.

"It's probably dysplasia," I said sadly.

"I'm afraid it is," she replied.

A dog two years old shouldn't have hip problems if they're well conformed and soundly bred. Dysplasia is a hip deformity that affects certain breeds of dogs very hard. It can show up in virtually all breeds, but it's rare. With our dogs we always test for hips, eyes and diseases before any breeding ever takes place, removing dogs that have problems from the gene pool. With some breeds like Labs and goldens, the problem is so acute that often breeders have just given up and breed whether the condition exists or not, passing the problem on to future dogs and owners. The British, who are notorious for this practice, rationalize it by saying, "We breed dogs according to their best characteristics. If they demonstrate the good traits, we breed to that; if any undesirable trait goes with it, well, that can be dealt with later."

The practical reality of that thinking is that if the undesirable dysplasia comes along with it, the owner has few choices. One is to let the dog live with it, which means by year five or six the dog will be unable to stand and will have to be put down; another option it to dispatch the dog, returning it to the breeder (if they offer a guarantee) and replace it with a new puppy. Finally, the dog can undergo surgery. My sister predictably chose this last route. Surgery usually costs $2,000 to $3,000 and requires a three-month recovery process, but it will usually carry the dog to 11 or 12 years of age. Had I requested a field test of Charles' two parents that fateful day, I could have probably detected the hip problems at the time.

My alarms should have gone off by the fact that the

breeders didn't offer an OFA certificate, but I was out of my element. Dysplasia can affect all dogs no matter how athletic they are, and it can be heartbreaking. I felt like such a rookie about this mess, but it was a lesson learned.

Charlie healed well and continued to be a terrific house dog. Occasionally he would venture on little hunting trips in his backyard. Relying on his instincts, he'd catch birds and mice mostly and proudly give them to the first person to show up. One day, Charlie arrived at the door with a much larger animal in his mouth, and Gerry let Charlie in to present it. With all the pride he could muster, looking much like his regal "distant cousin" Cent Von Esterfeld, Charlie presented to Gerry the dead animal. Uncertain even as to what it was, Gerry took it in hand, inspected it and realized it was an opossum. Thanking Charlie profusely and praising him for his hunting ability, he set the opossum on the floor of the dining room and gave Charlie a dog bone as a reward. Charlie enjoyed the bone and went out to bask in the sunshine of Southern California.

When Gerry returned to gather up the dead opossum, it was missing. He called out loud to see if Bonnie or Emily had come home and threw it out, but there was no answer. He wondered if Charlie had picked it up and taken it outside with him. He went out to where the contented dog was sleeping . . . without the opossum carcass. It occurred to Gerry that "playing possum" is more than an old expression and that he and his Midwestern hunting dog had been hoodwinked by this slick L.A. marsupial. Gerry woke Charlie, and armed with broom, dustpan and golden retriever, he ventured into opossum territory the way I would go forward with Jäger, Cent and my shotgun to harvest a meal. Charlie quickly struck a point at the hutch cabinet in the dining room, indicating life. Gerry maneuvered the broom under the cabinet in an effort to displace the opossum. The opossum evaded the attack, and Gerry displaced only collectible coffee cups from their perch in the cabinet, breaking their handles in the process.

"Sic 'em up, Charlie!" Gerry yelled, a command Charlie had never heard before. Gerry then got a hair dryer, and holding it like he was Dirty Harry gripping his gun, he moved from the bathroom through the living room and back to the dining room where the intruder lay. Plugging it in, he pulled the trigger to blast, blow or terrify the thing out into Charlie's waiting jaws.

The primary effect of the blast was to dislodge numerous dustballs and tufts of dog hair out from under the rarely moved piece of furniture on the hardwood floor. Charlie retreated quickly as the jetsam flew at him under the pressure of hot air. Gerry then decided that the best course was to lift and move the very heavy piece of furniture in the hope that it would create Charlie's chance to triumph. With a huge heave Gerry moved the hutch, causing more china to fall and break inside. The sound scared the opossum, and it dashed for new cover. With several leaps the golden retriever had regained his quarry and the opossum had apparently perished again.

In L.A. they release captured opossums. I'm not sure if that is a statute or tradition. They released this one by the swimming pool fence, probably where Charlie caught it in the first place.

Charlie is now twelve. The dysplasia surgery performed ten years ago has given him some very good years. While visiting California, we saw him struggle to stand up; we also saw him suddenly fall over. He lay there. He was hurt, embarrassed and confused, with a look that said, "What happened, boss? What just happened?"

He struggled to get up again, but he couldn't stay up. As they get old, the falling, instability and creakiness sets in. Sometimes, like in Charlie's case, it's the dysplasia problem combined with spinal pain that leads to the hind quarters giving out. It's actually the pain that causes the legs to go out. For other dogs the symptoms are similar, but an inflamed inner ear throws off the equilibrium. For still others it's the residue of a stroke-like problem that leads to confusion or loss of balance. Whatever the cause, it's an alarm that rings loud when you see your longtime pal, partner and teammate suffering like this. Many assume it's the end and fear that their next trip to the vet will be their last. Rarely, however, is that the case. Today there are pain-management products that can help reduce the effects of dysplasia even at fairly advanced stages. There are antibiotics for the balance and inner-ear problems and other things to help the confusion. It is, though, a wake-up call. While Charlie won't die today, he is probably down to his last nine to 15 months.

"You'll know when it's time," Kath has said for years. The indicators vary. Like when the storms scared Gus to the point he'd shiver in the corner writhing with fear or when Liesel leaked and didn't even know it. When Jäger was so creaky that even with the best painkillers she couldn't support her weight. When Mich couldn't get himself outside or stand on floors that were slippery. When Gretchen's tumor got so large you weren't able to look at it and it was clearly irritating her. When it sets in that one more treatment, protocol, surgery or set of medications is only because you would rather pay more money than face the terminal reality. All these are indications that it's time.

Never think these older dogs don't value some simple things as the time draws near. Take a little time and walk with them alone, on a leash, and talk to them as you go, like you used to do. Give them a little treat, make their food special. It's not like at this point it's going to kill them anyway. Let them have peace; don't let pups and younger, high-energy dogs abuse them. Remember that they are pack animals and will perceive the changing social order. Lift them when you otherwise wouldn't, help them if you can. A bath towel under the hind quarters lends a lot of support to bad hips. Don't bitch at them about leaks. They feel as bad as you do! It won't be long before they'll be gone and you'll need to throw that rug away anyway. Keep them away from the sights and sounds of storms the best you can. A windowless room in a basement or their dog crate inside your closed-up vehicle can help them through the bad weather. Lie with them on the floor and pet them, don't dwell on areas that are sore, painful or uncomfortable, but be close. Your dog knows and remembers your smells better than any other smell in the world.

When it is time, if you can do it, be with them. Hold them while the vet administers the shot. If you can do it in your own home, pick a favorite place, dog bed, couch or rug. This way, there's no anxiety about going into the vet's office, which some dogs fear.

Merry Maker, Jäger, Gretchen, Liesel, Gus and Bernie all perished just that way . . . at the right time.

SAD TIMES

We had just we learned of Bernie's kidney failure and the reality of it was sinking in. Bernie was languishing. We knew that he would vacillate between extreme sickness and relative health for a while, as long as his extra treatments were maintained. As she does, Kath had enlisted the aid of her doctor friend, Nancy, and nurse friend, Mary Jo. They supplied her and helped her give Bernie I.V. treatments that prolonged his life. As she had with Cent and Mixx, she brought modern medicine to dogs without regard to cost, practicality or even outcome. Bernie would learn to stand willingly as he was filled with needles and I.V. solutions, and sure enough, he'd feel better for several days afterward, but then his breath would get foul again and his energy would wane. The symptoms of renal failure for dogs and humans are very similar, and so is the treatment and Kath had become good at scrounging used medical supplies. No one in this process, however, deluded themselves as to what the eventual outcome would be.

Each morning I would go out for my morning exercise. We now lived right next door to the club and as part of my morning ritual the dogs and I would go through a small break in the club fence and enter the trail system, giving us access to over 600 acres at 6:30 in the morning before the business day begins. While Cent, Jäger and I would run every morning in the city when we were all younger, now the pack and I would run and walk throughout the land. For about two hours we'd go out and cover ground, all of us loving the tradition and invigorated by its process. We would go through the sporting clays courses to the club house, across the creek and into the hunting fields. We visited Challenge Field, Creek Bottom, Forest Bound, Middle Hill North, Urseth Crossing, climb the Big Hill to the 160 and then would find our way back along the Big Slough to the cut off. The dogs run, frolic, hunt, point, flush, catch birds at times and have a ball. We all do! I run, walk, lift weights, listen to the radio and watch sunrises which are inevitably beautiful, no matter the season. As I approach the house I always try to gather the pack up so everyone gets back together.

On this October morning, Haley (as she was prone to do) freelanced a little and took her own route. As I rushed to clean up that morning, the six dogs were in their kennel when there was a knock on the door. By the time I opened the door the person had left. Ten minutes later the phone rang; the person who had been knocking had gone to the club and now the club called to tell me that this guy had hit

Haley on the highway and that she was dead. The dog I suspected would be along any minute, who I had just "been out" with, was dead, hit by a car on a highway she never should have been close to. I was stung, sad and angry all at once. I had to call Kath and tell her. The call was very hard.

We had always assumed that Gus and Liesel who were born together, lived together for 13 years and had hunted, eaten, run and enjoyed each other, would depart around the same time. They had aged similarly, despite the sex difference, and while their ailments weren't the same, they were in about equal condition. Both leaked, creaked, had developed fears that they never had before and their joints weren't supporting them anymore. The dogs that had run so hard, so fast and for so long had slowed down. Gus, the great swimmer, was arthritic from the cold water he loved so much. Liesel was unsteady from the thousands of miles she had run through cover that tore at her body and joints and that she ignored completely to accomplish her singular objective.

Dr. John Bailey has cared for our dogs for over 25 years. He was a young man when we met and the vet who tied back to Jäger. His shorthair was her father, so he too is part of The Line. He came on an old-fashioned house call to give Gus and Liesel an injection that would painlessly cause them to pass on. I'm not good at this; Kath has become more of an expert than a person should have to be. With the dogs completely comfortable in their own home, their favorite place to be now that they're old, and with Kath calmly petting them, Dr. Bailey gave a little shot to Gus and Liesel, the last Jäger-Cent pups we had. A more beautiful boy than Gus would be hard to ever find, but he never became a breeder in The Line because of the tough decisions that we made.

Liesel had been a successful champion, winning numerous tournaments, state championships and placing in several U.S. Opens. She had been the Alpha in the pack, had inherited it from Jäger, reigned well then relinquished it to Abby. They were still, quiet, calm, genuinely content as the shots were given. There was no stirring or whining. The brother and sister sensed and felt each other. They had shared almost every day of the previous 13 years — now they would share this final experience. The pain would be gone, the ailments wouldn't matter. They would no longer be afraid of storms.

SAL

Sal was a very good-looking liver-ticked male German shorthair at the club kennel. He hunted with Mike Kretsch, the club guide who had nurtured and developed Abby and Hooty. I had enjoyed some really good performances with Sal in several tournaments, and I decided it would be good to bring him home to cheer things up a bit. I figured that a talented and spirited two-and-a-half-year-old who had the potential to become an important breeder in The Line would be good for everybody. When he arrived, he fit in quite well, though he was shy. When we'd go exercise in the morning, he'd tend to hang back and walk with me rather than frolic with the other dogs, racing and chasing like Fritz, Mixx and Abby loved to do.

I took him hunting one morning and after three hours he started to walk behind me. I thought he was sick or injured, but no he was just tired of hunting. I realized then that as talented as he was for tournaments, as good-looking as he was, as pleasant as he could be, Sal didn't fit in my life. It was very hard to move Sal back to the kennel because he liked living in the house, but he never blended into the pack and he wasn't tenacious enough for what I was doing. Mike Kretsch, Kristi, Terry — they were all disappointed. Kath understood because she had been through very difficult decisions before and knew that we only accept what we completely believe will be the best in every way to The Line. Sal would eventually be sold and end up in a wonderful home with a good man as his master.

I began to notice that Kath was crying frequently, for no apparent reason. She had always been so tough that it surprised me, but I thought it was mostly related to Bernie's ongoing treatments. In retrospect, I think it was cumulative — Haley gone, Gus and Liesel gone, Bernie sick. The thing that had consistently, for over 25 years, brought her so much pleasure, purpose and pride had now become a source of sadness. Finally, as she is so capable of doing, she knew it was time, and Doc Bailey ended Bernie's life, one that was so denied and cruelly cut short. She didn't really want to replace Bernie. "No puppies now," was the mantra.

ABBY'S DISAPPEARANCE

It was a very warm January morning, a Friday, and I had two interviews with prospective key personnel for the club. I was excited about the interviews and the possibility of working with these people. As always, the dogs and I piled out the door for our morning jaunt; Abby, Mixx, Fritz and I walking and running in the unseasonably temperate weather with melting snow and ice all around. It was a beautiful morning.

Abby ran with the speed and confidence that only a seven-year-old female pack leader can conjure. She had developed the ability to adjust her head's height and angle to the slightest scent or wind change, running with her head up on warm days when there was mud or melting snow, and with her head down on frozen ground.

She was so smart. She'd learned from trial and error, by observation, experience. She was trained and cared for, but most great dogs make themselves out of an intense desire to please. That morning she was the most awarded tournament hunting dog ever, having assembled 754 points in her career, outdistancing even some of the greats by hundreds of points, and she was at the top of her game. The state championships began the next day.

As she went, she was pointing first a pheasant, then a chukkar, then more pheasants. As she'd strike her points, Fritz would back her. When we returned to the clubhouse area, I called for the dogs to join up with me. We had become somewhat scattered. Usually, Abby would go ahead on a different path, Fritz would stay pretty close and Mixx would be a little behind the gang.

As I approached home, Fritz was the only one with me; as I continued to call for the other dogs, I circled back to the fence line and then headed back to the house because I needed to clean up for my meeting. When I had shaved and showered, I went out expecting to find Abby and Mixx at the door, but they weren't there so I jumped in my truck and headed to the club to look for them and attend my first meeting. At the club I didn't see them right away, but in no time Mixx was caught and tied up to a dog stake outside the clubhouse door — but still no Abby.

We had the meeting in the dining room that overlooks the Big Slough and the road that Abby would head down to go home. As we talked I gazed out the window, hoping to see her any minute. As soon as the first meeting was over I raced to my truck to get Mixx and to let Abby in the house, as I assumed she would be there waiting. To my surprise and disappointment, she wasn't. I then circled back to the club to meet with my second appointment, "I'm looking forward to meeting with you," I said, "but we need to talk in my truck 'cause I've got to search for my dog." It was about 11:00 a.m. and still no sign of her.

I drove every route I thought she could have taken and then I'd get out and call for her, knowing full well she knew the grounds better than any dog on earth; that third-mile from the Lodge to my house was her regular beat. She wasn't lost, I knew that, but where was she? I'd asked everyone I saw as I tried to focus on my business conversation, but my mind was on Abby. I continued to search, call her name, visit and re-visit places where she could be. At dark my hopes were crushed and the gravity of the situation sunk in. Abby was missing.

Since we have surveillance cameras on the club parking lot, I now began to view the tapes, and from them we could clearly see that she was near the clubhouse up to 11:00 a.m. or so; that was the last time she was on the tape. We deduced that she had vanished somewhere between the clubhouse and The Hunter's Lodge. I studied every vehicle that entered or left the club for the next one and a half hours, everyone being a lead in a missing dog incident. Finally, I knew I had to tell Kath what was happening. When she answered the phone her voice was clear and had the confidence for which she's famous. It would be the last time I'd hear that voice for some time. We'd lost Haley in the auto accident, Gus and Liesel to age, Bernie to renal failure and now Abby was missing — losing five dogs in less than a year was more than most people could possibly take.

To find Abby we posted a $1,000 reward. We notified all law enforcement in the 5-County area, posted alerts on all our websites. We made posters and placed them all over the countryside. Every trick that I had ever used as a boy would move into action and new ones that Kath would bring, widened the search zone. With a $1,000 reward there were young kids out searching everywhere, walking roadsides and calling Abby's name in swamps and forests.

We got phone calls — some helpful, some confusing, some misleading. The magic call we had received when Jäger went missing so many years before was not coming. We would review the surveillance tapes and study every vehicle that entered or left the property that afternoon. Kath would call dozens of vets' offices because Abby had an implanted chip and the hope, of course, was that someone would bring her in for care.

A listing on Craig's List would lead to some conmen who wanted to sell information on the dog's whereabouts. With no information to offer they were unmasked before any money was lost. A private detective was hired and old friends in law enforcement were called for any thoughts they might have. More and more hours would be spent now by Kath on stakeouts and plot schemes. She was obsessed with finding Abby. I needed to get back on the road, but we'd talk every day. For an hour or more she'd repeat over and over what she was doing, had done and would do next. At one point she resorted to Reiki therapy in an attempt to alleviate her obsession, but it led to nowhere.

About two weeks after Abby went missing, we estimated that we had over 500 people either looking for her or who were at least keeping an eye out. As is always the case it's hard to keep the flame burning that actively and people began to give up. I was giving up, too, but Kath was even more intense and was not weakening in her resolve at all.

I then broached the topic of another dog or puppy. "You know we have some great dogs in the kennel right now, and one of 'em would love to come here to the house. Some of them are even Abby's daughters — Maddy, Ellie or Sugar. What do you think?"

"I'm not ready and I don't know if I'll ever be ready. My heart is broken." Kath began to cry. "I don't think I'll ever love another dog like that. Jäger I could handle. She had a full life and our relationship was complete. Abby is only seven and she should be here another seven years. I just wasn't ready. I've lost too much, five dogs in eight months is too much to lose. I don't think I could ever open up to another dog again." She wouldn't stop crying for over half an hour. It was clear she wasn't ready.

Overriding everything in her grief was the disbelief that someone would actually be so cruel as to take Abby.

"Why would someone do this to us?" she'd ask again and again. "Why would someone do this? How could they be so cruel?" She knew how we had always worked to return lost dogs. She knew of Duke, remembered Dirk, and worked hard to help get the old Lab we'd found on the road a safe future. She simply couldn't believe someone to be so callous.

I, on the other hand, remembered Dirk the Dog and Axel, how wanton and self-centered the thieves were, how close we were to losing the Ottman that cold night, how Jäger was nearly lost to us at such a young age. Had we not answered the phone on that one call the woman made, we may have never seen her again. People find it easy to rationalize keeping a found dog. "Poor dog, it must need a home. Oh, I can help you, puppy, I can help you," and so it begins. I remembered how Jeff got his Irish setter, "It's my guardian angel"

— these kinds of rationalizations don't work with a horse, a watch or a car. It's especially difficult to understand when the dog in question is licensed, has multiple tags, contact information, even microchips to further identify the animal. Some people just don't get it — that to many people, the contents of their home are just possessions, no matter how valuable, but dogs are irreplaceable members of the family.

Sadly, the appearance on the surveillance tape was the last we'd ever see of our Abby. We never found her.

Without Abby, Fritz and Mixx became the Geezers. They just got old; the fun was out of their lives too. The little spark plug that ran the show, entertained them, cuddled with them, played, taunted and licked them was gone. The doghouse roof was empty.

IT'S A SMALL WORLD

Since the creation of many dog breeds are a collaboration of effort by similarly minded people throughout the world, it shouldn't be a surprise that The Line has become as international as it has. As an example, the Labrador retriever was created by Maritime-oriented hunters and fishermen to work in cold water and difficult circumstances, but Labs would never have reached their broad appeal without the breeders, promoters and markets of England and North America's more southern climes. While the poodle may be a product of France, its market and popularity is worldwide. Even some of the very narrow breeds with very local origins, like the large Munsterlander or French Brittany, have found their way to North America and other locales around the globe.

So it is as well with The Line. In its truest sense, it began internationally with a German-born sire and an American dam. As the generations have passed, I realize that we now have placed pups all over the world and that their progeny hunt and wander ground foreign to their ancestors, their littermates and their cousins. We've shipped pups and dogs to Alaska, California, Connecticut, Hawaii, Massachusetts, Texas, numerous Midwestern states, Canadian provinces, Africa and Venezuela. Some of these families continue to keep us posted on the progress of their dogs and their achievements at home or in the field.

Once as I was walking down a crowded aisle at the Shot Show in Orlando, I was unsuspectingly bear hugged into submission by a huge Polynesian fellow who recognized me and realized I had sent him his two favorite dogs. The duo no longer hunted pheasants in deep January snow like their littermates, because they now worked on a preserve on the Big Island of Hawaii and sought pheasant, quail and partridge in the volcanic soils and lush beauty.

As will happen at a sports bar in Montreal, I struck up a conversation with a fellow who also loved hockey. Soon the conversation moved to dogs and he became downright cocky as he relayed the exploits, heroics and accomplishments of his dog. I listened silently to each story, smiling and nodding and enjoying the tales. Finally, I asked him where he had gotten this fabulous dog.

"In the United States, a place called the Minnesota Horse and Hunt club," he said.

I smiled and introduced myself. He was so excited that he said, "Don't move. Whatever you do, don't move. I'll be right back."

He dashed to the door and in ten minutes returned with his wife and dog, which he brought right into the bar, despite protests from the hostess and waitress.

He merely explained, "This is very important. It's a family reunion and we can't be bothered by silly laws."

I found myself frolicking on the floor of the bar with his dog that was as social and friendly as Jäger or Abby. While I hadn't seen the dog since it was eight weeks old, I knew how it wanted to be greeted, stroked, held, where to tease its ears and massage its head. I wasn't allowed to buy another drink the rest of the night and even my dinner was on him. When the police finally showed up to remove the canine crasher from the bar, we all left rather than stay without him, as he was the one who had brought us all so close together.

CHEVY

When she first arrived she was just an "outcross," a female dog that wasn't part of The Line, but could become an important breeder for the males of The Line. Every few years we bring in these dogs to freshen up The Line and make certain we aren't just line breeding. While there are strong advocates of line breeding, and we've certainly done it ourselves over the years to great success, the practice tends to exaggerate a line's weaknesses as well as its strengths, often in the same breeding — making for stars and duds in the same litter. As a result, we use outcrosses on a regular basis to breed for consistency in each litter and each dog. The "little girl" was whiter than we usually liked; she was kind of shy and while we liked her pedigree, we didn't see great talent in her right away.

Rather than have her languish in the kennel, Bob Burditt and Kristi Johnson, both longtime employees at the club, offered to take the dog home to socialize her, which they did very effectively. Within months she was assertive, physically larger and began to develop a pert little personality that even included a rare dog ability — she smiles. The expression involves a lifting of her lips to expose her teeth, but not at all in a snarly way. It is undeniably a friendly smile.

We christened her Chevy, and she was the first pointing dog ever allowed to be in the check-in area. She would be exposed to dozens of people every day, sometimes hundreds. In the process she was getting more socialization than most pups achieve in a lifetime. Kristi would train her in simple tricks, discipline and then hunting. She learned fast, retained what she learned and adopted a queenly air about her. By the time she was one year old, she was becoming "Her Majesty."

I ran her myself in her first tournament, at the Iowa State Pheasant Championship, and while she demonstrated some promise, it was basically an inauspicious start. Bob and Kristi took her everywhere in her second year and the good-looking, smiling queen began to think that in God's order, people, dogs and Chevy were three separate species. She identified more with people than with the other dogs and liked them much better. As can be the case in sports or life in general, breaks happen and they sometimes create new opportunities. If Tom Brady wasn't injured, would the world have ever known how good Matt Cassel really is? If William McKinley hadn't been shot, would the country have ever experienced Teddy Roosevelt?

The day that Abby went missing was the Friday before the Minnesota State Pheasant Championship. Just barely seven years old, Abby would have had at least two of her best years still in front of her. Just the month before she had won the Menz Player's Championship with ease. When I had made out the entries for the State Tilt, I hadn't even entered Chevy. I knew that there were good reports from the fall hunting season and her guiding, but she wasn't even on the tournament roster. Now suddenly with Abby's disappearance, there was an opening for a one-and-three-quarter-year-old female German shorthair pointer named Chevy in both the Puppy and Pro Class. Any doubt about her readiness vanished when she hit the field.

The main issue with the competitors who would run her (like Matt and Tim Herold, Bruce Wohlrabe, Jim Miller, Rich Boumeester and Chris Slavik) was that she sported a pink collar and her toenails were painted pink on all four legs. Kristi made Chevy as girly as she could and it had become part of her character.

"I'm not running with a dog with painted-pink toenails," they would bluster. My only response was simple.

"I'm going to ask you to do it once. If after one run you don't want to run with her ever again, I'll understand."

Not one person ever complained about her nails or her pink collar ever again. There was so much talent there, bird desire and biddability that we could have dressed her up in a polka-dot skirt and these gruff and grumpy teammates would have gone for it.

By the end of the 2007 season she would be the high-point puppy, high-point dog and Dog of the Year. It was certain that she was in the right slot, and while Abby was sorely missed,

Chevy eased a little of the pain.

By springtime people were asking me, "Why don't you bring Chevy home to help ease the loss of Abby?" As much as I had come to love Chevy and appreciate her ability, I knew that it would just transfer pain from one household to another with very little gain. Bob and Kristi had grown so attached to Chevy that it would have broken their hearts and I feared to move her. Much of her growth was due to their efforts and most of the strength of The Line is due to careful alliances that place great dogs in great households for their entire lives — the challenging puppy years, the exciting halcyon productive years and the aging, descending quiet years before death. This careful placement system is essential to always having the best talent available.

Besides, Kath was still in her undiagnosed depression and while Chevy was the one dog she might have wanted around, she still wasn't ready for dogs or even the remote risk of heartbreak. Whenever I needed a dog for hunting, Kristi would willingly send Chevy with me, and we had become great friends in the process. With me, some things were different, though. I'd make Chevy ride in a kennel, sleep on the floor of a motel room or at the farm (most of the time!) and not let her whine, which she was prone to do if she didn't get her way. Whenever I was with her, she would remove some of the ache of Abby's absence, but she also reminded me how fragile things are. In the morning she would rest her head on the bed next to my face and just look at me, not making a sound until I woke up, just like Abby did. Then I would find myself talking to her in sentences, something I'd never done before, even with my smartest dogs like Jäger and Abby.

"Chevy, go lie down on your own bed," I would say. If I said, "Chevy, go lie down," she would jump up on my bed and lie down. No other dog had ever differentiated that simple command so cleverly.

"No, Chevy, we will not be going hunting today," I say when I enter the check-in and she comes running with a smile to say hello, hoping that we were going hunting.

"We will go hunting tomorrow. You and I will go hunting tomorrow." I'd almost feel silly talking to a dog in sentences, but I didn't really care what others thought, just that she understood me.

KATH

As the days passed after Abby's disappearance, Kath was more and more sullen, prone to crying spells and unable to focus. She was obsessed with the surveillance tapes that we had and from the day Abby disappeared she studied them for hours and hours on her computer. She developed suspects and ideas, theories and rationales as to who would have done it and why. With every phone call her hopes would momentarily soar and then fall when she'd hit a dead end.

Once she got to the point where she had some prime suspects, she would begin to stake out their homes and look for clues that might lead to Abby. This would lead to five prime suspects and over a dozen stakeouts. She would contact vet offices because Abby was microchipped and she hoped they'd find her when the thief brought her in for vet work or just a check-up. The vets in certain areas were prime prospects for follow-up calls. Most people, along with most of the police officers and sheriff department personnel she contacted, were kind to Kath during this time, offering sympathy and sometimes advice.

She spent most of her nights sleepless, lying in the fetal position, crying herself to sleep, only to wake up to another round of tears. She withdrew from everything except work, where she was still okay. Once work was over, though, her obsession would return and the deep sadness took over. As much as I missed Abby, I had really lost them both because Kath's pain made it so difficult to be around her.

I was on the road a lot, but when we talked she began to say things like, "I'll never smile again until we find Abby," and "I don't think I'll every be happy if we don't find her," and "Without her my life is basically over." These comments frightened me and those around her. The grief had swallowed up her entire life. The stake-outs were lasting six and eight hours in winter weather. Neighbors began to wonder who was lurking around and why, calling the police and security companies. Her singular purpose was to find her dog and she was careful to not cross the line of legal behavior, but she did stray close to it.

After three months I thought things might improve, but they didn't. Kath just became more zealous, and she began to be angry with me that I wasn't working as hard at searching as she was. Her despair was deeper than anything I have ever encountered. We were unable to talk about anything else. One day, after about four full months, I was on the road and we were talking by phone. She had spoken about the situation for a half-hour when I suddenly said, "I'll listen to three more minutes about Abby, but then that's it. You have to talk about something else."

Most conversations I'd set a time limit, five minutes or maybe ten, and then no more talk about Abby. It had to end. The time limits seemed to help. It forced her to talk about other things and not dwell or obsess. Even though things were better, she swore she'd never laugh or be happy again until Abby showed up.

It was about then that Maddy (Abby's daughter from her first litter) gave birth to pups. There has never been a better assessor of litters than Kath, but she wouldn't even take a look.

CHEVY-BEAU

When it finally came time for Chevy to make her addition to The Line, it was decided that Beau would be the sire. He was from the core of The Line. He traced back to Jäger-Cent, Mich, Willy and Gretchen. He was a remarkably cold-nosed dog that could find birds in the worst conditions. He was very dark (liver, we call it), big, strong and a real lover boy. He had lived with Bruce since he was two. His hunt desire was exceptional, which had worked against Bruce several times. Once, notably when he had shot his limit of ducks too quickly on an opening day and was now forced to leave the field, Beau thought otherwise and dashed off. Bruce couldn't get him back; the day became long and he grew fearful.

"What should I do?" he asked me.

"Wait till dusk. If he hasn't shown up by then, we'll go to the logical places and holler and shoot until he shows up." Unfortunately, I had experience with just this problem from previous exploits. Once dark sets in, dogs have a different mentality. At about 6:30 p.m. (an hour and a half before dark) Bruce called home and told Lori and the girls, "Beau is missing." They all shared a tear. At 8:00 p.m. three groups headed out to three separate locations where Beau was most likely to show up. Spread over five square miles we would all start to call his name, honk horns and fire shots into the air, all things that are likely to cause a lost dog to show up. After ten minutes in the darkness my cell phone rang.

"Beau is found!" were the welcome words on the other end of the line. Jim Knutson, our old friend, had found him along the road when he was heading over to Rebel Lodge.

Beau was exhausted when I got there. He couldn't stand up, so we put water with electrolytes in front of his face. He lapped it up. Then we fed him treats, not pushing too much on him. He had been gone about ten hours on a warm day, but he was alive, well and being cared for. Bruce called Lori and the girls to tell them everything was okay.

I was very confident that the Beau-Chevy breeding was going to be a classic breeding and very successful. At about the same time we had also bred Maddy, who was an Abby pup from her first litter, with Ringo, out of the core of our Line. This litter was well subscribed for and I had high hopes of getting a pup myself, if Kath could just get through it. I didn't even dream that I might get a "pick pup" out of both litters. Not since I was a kid when we just couldn't have a dog had I been so "dogless" and my prospects so bleak. Oh sure, the Geezers — Mixx and Fritz — were around, but

Mixx, of course, couldn't find a bird and Fritz, now 13, was deaf.

Maddy, like her mother, took great care of her litter, as would Chevy when hers came. Only two months apart, these dogs were the culmination of 30 years of building The Line. They were the offspring of tough decisions, of weeding out talented dogs in deference to dogs with even more talent, of eliminating dogs not because they weren't talented, but because of defects or diseases that were no fault of their own. These dogs were the progeny of quiet, thoughtful nights and long, fun-filled, grueling days in the field assessing who really were the best and why. They were also the result of choosing dogs that were good with people, were easily socialized and had a loving side that made them special.

TOR

After all the efforts, hopes and assistance to find Abby, it was becoming clear that whoever had her intended to keep her and that she wasn't coming home easily. I was clearly trying to move forward, but Kath was still locked in the past and didn't seem able to move on. Then we got the call about Tor. He had won The Top Dog Show-down in 2005, was a true champion and a top notch native bird dog. He was now ten.

Tor had enjoyed the run of the place his entire life. He lived on Matt's farm and enjoyed the life Matt had envisioned for him on that day of the draft almost ten years earlier. Tor had seen his father Mitch pass on, lost a kennel-mate to the nearby county road, watched his pal and cousin Jolt get shipped off because Matt so feared that his roving would lead to him getting hit by a car as well. Tor had sired one of the most anticipated litters in the history of The Line with Abby and, not surprisingly, it was outstanding. Now Rock, a descendant from that litter, joined him on the farm. The old Geezer and the less-than-year-old grand-pup got along well. Tor taught Rock his favorite haunts for raccoons, mice, rats, skunks and weasels. Of course, he also showed him how to hunt pheasant and quail. Rock would run along and follow the master.

When a young dog with an unrefined but developing nose follows an old salt like Tor, even though he can't smell everything or can't discriminate the nuances of scent, he learns to associate as they go and this makes him better. I've seen how Jäger helped Gretchen, Mich helped Fritz, Fritz helped Abby and Tor helps Rock. Good dogs train each other.

It was a cold December day and all the ponds had frozen up, leaving no escape for two mute swans, several geese and a couple of domestic ducks. Matt had installed an aerator to keep the pond behind his barn open for the birds. While the birds swam quietly in the 30-yard circle that the aerator maintained, mink came silently, as they do. Mink are one of the few of God's creatures that hunt for fun. They will cut their victim's throats from the front or the back, lick some blood and then kill again and again — all for the sport of it.

As we would later piece together from tracks, scratches and evidence, Tor and Rock were on patrol, as they always were, when the stir began. A mink was chasing the ducks, but all the birds were affected because of the small amount of water available. Mink are excellent swimmers above and below the water. They fear nothing except people and dogs. Tor went to the ruckus, Rock followed. He evidently saw the mink going after the ducks and went out onto the ice. He moved to the edge when the ice broke and he fell into the frozen pond. The mink scurried away, leaving some injured birds. Tor now tried to crawl out of the water, his claws unable to gain traction on the ice. Matt had gone to town for a brief while. Tor swam in circles, trying again and again to gain a foothold on the slippery surface to get himself out of the pond. A dog has about 20 minutes to get himself out of ice water before hypothermia sets in and he drowns. Rock barked and howled, yipped and whined. He circled the pond, afraid for Tor, but unable to help. As Matt pulled into the drive he could hear Rock's anguished cries. These were sounds he had never heard from a dog before. He quickly moved to the pond and saw the distraught Rock at the water's edge and the lifeless Tor floating on top of the water. He retrieved Tor's body, which was still malleable, and tried to expel the water from his lungs. For over 20 minutes, Matt worked to bring back the first pick of ten years ago — but to no avail. Tornado Schnormado was dead and The Line had lost one of its greats.

HANK

In **May, Maddy (Abby's daughter** from her first litter) delivered a litter of beautiful pups. They were Abby-Cowboy on one side and Ringo from the core of The Line on the other. This meant the litter traced back to Jäger-Cent, Mich and Johne.

Kath brought it up. She was willing to look. She wasn't making any promises, but she would at least look.

There was a male who just ran the puppy box. He was strong and smart, he slept little, he always had the best teat and he wreaked havoc on the others. Kath's eye for puppies is without peer. She watches litters for hours and studies how they interact with each other and their surroundings. After careful observation, she accurately predicts the personalities, strengths and weaknesses of the litter, while most people can't even tell one pup from another. Many times as she watched this litter, she had to wipe tears from her eyes, and she was unable and unwilling to talk to or be seen by other people.

"Do you have a favorite?" she asked me at about week six.

"Yes," I said, immediately hoping this could lead somewhere. "The big male with the brown head. He's special."

"He sure is," she said. "He's a hellion and he's so Abby I can hardly stand to watch him, it makes me so sad."

Realizing this was probably another no, I backed off some and said, "We could always keep him at the club and see how it goes."

She bit her lip and nodded. More tears came. Unlike in my childhood when I plotted, connived and opportunistically asked for a puppy whenever I could, I knew this was different. I didn't push, but I did want that dog.

Days later, the conversation started innocently. "If we were to get a dog, what would we call it?" she asked.

Now that was the best question I'd been asked in years. It sounded like the door was suddenly open or at least unlocked. I had been working on names for a week and said, "Heinrich, but we call him Hank."

"I like that," she said, and I knew the little spitfire was coming home and that Hank would have a chance to become a hunting dog who would bring cheer into a house that had been without it for way too long.

HANK AND SCENT

When I took Hank at eight weeks to the Youth Hunt Camp, I knew the boys at the camp would accelerate his socialization. He was cocky and confident, the pick of the litter to both Kath's eye and mine. We run the camp for four weeks each summer, when about ten kids per session arrive at the club and live there for the week. We teach them to hunt. They shoot 75 to 100 rounds of shotgun per day, 100 to 200 rounds of rifle and pistol, they learn to track, set decoys, build deer stands, climb trees, walk in swamps, work in the dark and they go on an actual hunt. They shoot birds, clean birds, cook birds and eat them. They learn to identify flora and fauna and, hopefully, they have a lot of fun. Ultimately, that's what it's all about.

The boys were down in the lake swimming, canoeing and roughhousing, and I brought the tiny Hank down to the water. My hope was that he would step in the water a little bit, nothing more. He walked to the lake's edge, put a foot into the water and never hesitated, he just kept right on going — past some of the boys and on to others. When he was about 50 yards out I was incredulous and said, "He's not afraid of anything." He kept going and was soon out over 100 yards with no sign of slowing down. This less-than-ten-pound pup swam out to 200 yards, at which point I yelled, "Hank! Come here, Hank." He turned around, swam on in and shook off. The boys gathered round and cheered him for his prowess. He loved the swim and cherished the attention.

For the rest of the summer he would be at my side and with the kids of the camp. The boys and girls played with him; he wrassled, kissed and ran with them. When they fired shotguns, rifles and pistols, he stayed at their feet, with no fear of the noise or muzzle blasts. Hank believed he was one of the gang, and he was constantly held and passed from kid to kid. His socialization was as good as any dog's I've ever seen; he was always pushed, always loved, always cheered and always making others feel good at the same time.

Once Hank was home and settled in, it was time for him and me to spend some quality time getting to know each other. When puppies are eight to 12 weeks old, they're small and cuddly. While we had been spending good outdoor time in the water, around shooting, with lots of exercise and socialization at the camp, we also needed some time — just him and me. This typically came at the end of the day. I'd bring Hank into bed with me until he'd fall asleep. As I held him, I told him stories like I would to a little kid. Of course I knew he didn't understand what I was saying, but neither would a very young child. He seemed to like the sound of my voice and the closeness we shared. I actually enjoyed telling the stories, because they brought back such great memories.

"Oh Hank," I'd begin. "Do you know how lucky you are to come from such a great line of dogs? Do you know that your great-great-grandmother Jäger won the U.S. Open with only one eye and 23 pellets in her head? Yes she did, Hank, yes she did. Do you know that at one time your Uncle Gus was so small that he could lie here with me just like you are right now? Oh yeah, he wasn't always 80 pounds. At one time he was little just like you. Do you know that one year he retrieved 360 ducks? Yep. That's a lot of ducks, isn't it? Speaking of ducks, do you know that your great-grandfather Mich went all the way to the Delta Marsh to hunt ducks? He was there with the Labs and Chesapeakes. Do you think you could ever do that, Hank?"

He rolled over and I rubbed his belly.

"Oh Hank, do you know that Uncle Fritz could find a bird in a 50 mile-an-hour wind with the barometer dropping? Well he could and Beau can too. Do you know that your grandmother Abby would be very nice to you if she were here today, do you know that? She could hunt alright. That dog could hunt, Hank. If you're 80 percent of her, you'll be a great champion. Oh Hank, if Mr. Cent could see you out there with me chasing those birds and swimming already at your age, he'd be mighty proud, Hank. Do you know he flew across an entire ocean to be here? Did you know that? Yep Hank, he might have been the best-lookin' dog ever until you showed up."

Hank yawned and stretched.

"Are you getting tired, Hank? Do you know that Uncle Willy won the state championship when he was only ten months old? Do you think you could ever do that? Great-grandpa Mich won three U.S. Opens. Did you know that? Well, it's true."

I just kept talking, yapping and sharing with Hank a history he would never know in a language he'd never comprehend, but I loved remembering those who preceded him. Then I told him the story about Roy Rogers and Cent and how Cent ate all the cheese and the deer hearts and the moose liver, and outside the bedroom door I heard something I hadn't heard in over a year. I heard an eavesdropper laughing out loud. When I looked she was gone, but it was unmistakable, and I knew that Hank had brought that laughter back into the house after such a long absence. The next morning Hank would rise at 5:00 a.m., well before the other dogs. In no time, though, he rallied the others to action to begin a new day.

Shortly after, when Kath actually said, "Let's get another one," I knew she had made it over the top of her depression. Hank had been a big part of the cure, and despite his moments of incorrigible activity, he was largely a joy.

There was never a moment of doubt as to which pup we would take from Chevy's litter, we only questioned what to call him. We decided on Scent. It had been a long time since we'd used that great name and all it meant and stood for. By adding the 'S' to Cent, we both anglicized the name and paid respect to Cent Von Esterfeld or Mr. Cent.

We now had two dogs with common predecessors, but with their own personalities and distinctions. One was whiter, one was darker. Scent looked more like Beau than Chevy,

Hank looked more like Abby than Ringo. The two fought, wrassled and teased each other, and they tormented the Geezers whose lives were blissfully dull before this pair showed up. Now their lives are punctuated with jaw games, bone searches and dominance pranks that remind you how much energy puppies really have.

One day, I heard the barking as I pulled into the driveway. The Geezers were making sounds I hadn't heard in years. I glanced at the kennel and did a double take. There in front of my eyes was Hank, the grandson of Abby, firmly and soundly standing on the doghouse roof, parading as only his grandmother could, with no way of knowing this was exactly what she did. Then he tore a shingle off the doghouse roof and tossed it to his amazed audience that included Fritz, Mixx and little Scent who kept trying to jump up there, but couldn't. Every day from then on, Hank would wake up at five o'clock in the morning, ready to go no matter the season or the amount of light. He was now the alpha, and when I'd see him, my spirit would lift and a smile would come to my face.

Between the two of them, they chewed up hundreds of dollars of dog doors, destroyed dozens of dog beds, tore the shingles off the doghouse roof, tunneled beneath the kennel fence, gnawed on a dozen pairs of boots and shoes and ate the dog collars right off the Geezers' necks. They jumped up seven feet to ransack everything we'd carefully stored on shelves above the kennel. They have learned to point birds, retrieve them, honor the other's point and can run lickety-split all day long. There are times when I watch them and I see Abby. I see Jäger when one of them pivots on their nose while going full speed and their entire body flows around from the momentum, but their nose doesn't move. There are times I see Mich, Willy and, of course, Cent, when the big brown Scent floats through a field so effortlessly. The apple doesn't fall far from the tree. There are people who just love dogs and there are people who love what dogs can do — I am the latter.

EPILOGUE – U.S. OPEN '09

As the 2009 U.S. Open Pheasant championship approached, Sieger — the defending Top Dog Showdown winner — was now five years old and in excellent shape. He had enjoyed a great season and was guaranteed a berth in the 2009 Top Dog Showdown. Sieger was an Abby pup from the Abby-Cowboy litter, a full brother and littermate to Toby and Maddy, Hank's mother. He was "Uncle Sieger" to Hank and they mostly got along very well. He was about to move into the breeding pool, and with his sculpted muscular body, he was as handsome as any dog in The Line. On Sunday, March 15, 2009, when Sieger would have normally been with the team at the Iowa State Pheasant Championship, he was hit by a car and killed. He had stayed behind because he had already earned his way into The Showdown.

The news struck me like a physical blow. He had been our number one team dog all year. He held several state championships and was the defending Top Dog champion. The disappointment and sadness ran deep as I made phone calls to team members Tim, Matt, Andrew, Jim, Chris and the others. All were devastated and shocked.

When the season began, Hank was the fourth-ranked dog on the U.S. Team in the Pro Class. (This put him at the bottom of the team.) As a puppy, it was unusual for him to be on the Pro Team in the first place, but Mia had turned nine and was now too old and, of course, Abby was still missing. Hank had enjoyed a good season, though, as a Pro; he had stopped competing at all as a puppy, and at only 16 months old was leading the Open Class for total points. With Sieger's death and his own strong season, Hank had earned himself a slot in the six-dog Showdown. Hank would now have to compete against the best-of-the-best for over $4,000 in prize money and the Top Dog trophy.

The day was marked by swirling winds and cold, unmoving temperatures. All the dogs struggled — flushers and pointers — to find birds. As Sieger lay cold in his grave, only two weeks after his accident, young Hank went to the starting line. On April 6, 2009, the puppy Hank won the Top Dog Showdown, beating the best. All the other pointers found five birds or less, while Hank found eight and stopped the clock in 11 minutes. He was the first and only puppy ever to win the Showdown. On that day he ran with the dignity of Cent Von Esterfeld and the speed of his grandmother Abby. He held his head like Willy and shifted to air-scent like Mich. His nose was cold like Gretchen's, and the dog that he had lived with almost every day of his life, Uncle Fritz, had shown him how to hunt in bad conditions. He moved with the quickness of Jäger and he looked almost as handsome as Uncle Sieger.

Now everyone knows that telling dogs about their predecessors is silly. Everyone knows that dogs don't understand sentences or human language, whether you speak English, Russian, French, Japanese, German or Portuguese. Everyone agrees that bedtime stories for dogs are ridiculous and a total waste of time — everyone that is, except me.

THE LINE

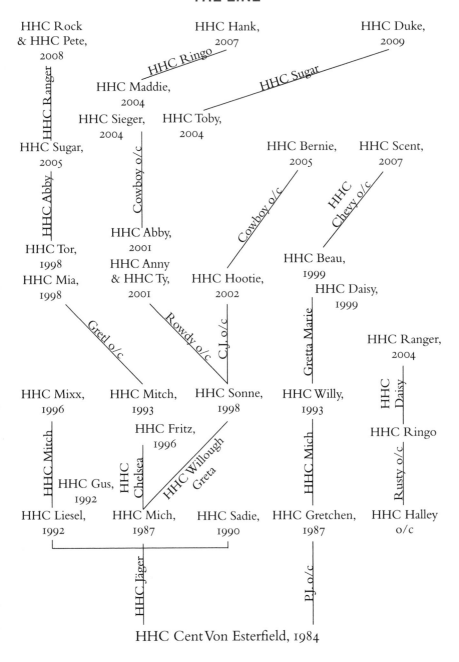

HHC Rock & HHC Pete, 2008

HHC Hank, 2007

HHC Duke, 2009

HHC Ranger

HHC Ringo

HHC Maddie, 2004

HHC Sugar

HHC Sieger, 2004

HHC Toby, 2004

HHC Sugar, 2005

HHC Bernie, 2005

HHC Scent, 2007

HHC Abby

Cowboy o/c

Cowboy o/c

HHC Chevy o/c

HHC Abby, 2001

HHC Tor, 1998

HHC Anny & HHC Ty, 2001

HHC Beau, 1999

HHC Mia, 1998

HHC Hootie, 2002

HHC Daisy, 1999

Gretl o/c

Rowdy o/c

CJ o/c

Gretta Marie

HHC Ranger, 2004

HHC Daisy

HHC Mixx, 1996

HHC Mitch, 1993

HHC Sonne, 1998

HHC Willy, 1993

HHC Ringo

HHC Fritz, 1996

HHC Willough Greta

HHC Chelsea

HHC Mitch

HHC Mich

Rusty o/c

HHC Gus, 1992

HHC Liesel, 1992

HHC Mich, 1987

HHC Sadie, 1990

HHC Gretchen, 1987

HHC Halley o/c

HHC Jäger

PJ o/c

HHC Cent Von Esterfield, 1984